THE WALTER LYNWOOD FLEMING
LECTURES IN SOUTHERN HISTORY
Louisiana State University

Other Published Lectures in This Series

The Repressible Conflict, 1830–1861
AVERY O. CRAVEN

Three Virginia Frontiers
THOMAS PERKINS ABERNETHY

South America and Hemisphere Defense
J. FRED RIPPY

The Plain People of the Confederacy
BELL IRVIN WILEY

Behind the Lines in the Southern Confederacy
CHARLES W. RAMSDELL

Lincoln and the South
J. G. RANDALL

The Rural Press and the New South
THOMAS D. CLARK

Plain Folk of the Old South
FRANK LAWRENCE OWSLEY

Confederate Leaders in the New South
WILLIAM B. HESSELTINE

The Texas Revolution
WILLIAM C. BINKLEY

Myths and Realities
CARL BRIDENBAUGH

The South Lives in History
WENDELL HOLMES STEPHENSON

Civil War in the Making, 1815–1860
AVERY O. CRAVEN

The Fall of Richmond
REMBERT W. PATRICK

The First South
JOHN RICHARD ALDEN

The Mind of the Old South
CLEMENT EATON

F.D.R. and the South
FRANK FREIDEL

Religious Strife on the Southern Frontier
WALTER BROWNLOW POSEY

The Politics of Reconstruction, 1863–1867
DAVID DONALD

Three Carpetbag Governors
RICHARD N. CURRENT

The Slave Power Conspiracy
and the Paranoid Style

DAVID BRION DAVIS

The Slave Power Conspiracy and the Paranoid Style

LOUISIANA STATE UNIVERSITY PRESS
BATON ROUGE

For Jeremiah

Acknowledgments

I wish to thank the Graduate School and the Department of History of Louisiana State University for the invitation to deliver the Walter Lynwood Fleming Lectures in Southern History, Thirtieth Series, 1969, which formed the substance of this book. I am deeply grateful to Mr. Joel Bernard, Mrs. Catharine S. McCalmon, and Mrs. Ellen Lundell for providing extensive assistance in research. I am also obliged to Mrs. Lundell for typing the manuscript. The staff of the Cornell University Library was particularly helpful in tracking down materials and in obtaining photocopies from other libraries.

Contents

1 *Images of Conspiracy in the Slavery Controversy: Conceptual Problems and Theoretical Framework*   3

2 *Polarization: The Abolitionists as Subversives; The Slave System Impregnable to the Word of Truth* 32

3 *The Slave Power and the Great American Enemy*   62

Notes   87

The Slave Power Conspiracy
and the Paranoid Style

1

Images of Conspiracy in the Slavery Controversy: Conceptual Problems and Theoretical Framework

As Richard Hofstadter has shown, Americans have frequently perceived the national political scene illuminated by the lurid glare of paranoid visions.[1] When the familiar political landscape, with all its party loyalty and logrolling compromise, has been reflected in chiaroscuro, even the most innocent shapes have assumed an ominous meaning. For in the eyes of paranoid alarmists, the very normality of society's surface conceals a gigantic conspiracy that has begun to control the course of history and subvert the values of Christianity and democracy. After free institutions miraculously survived the insidious plots of the British crown, they have supposedly been threatened by conspiracies of the French Illuminati, of Federalist oligarchs, of Freemasons, of the money power, of the Catholic Church, of the Slave Power, of foreign anarchists, of Wall Street bankers, of Bolsheviks, of internationalist Jews, of Fascists, of Communists, and of Black Pow-

3

er. Hofstadter suggests that a latent tendency to perceive the world in paranoid terms has been periodically aroused by sudden conflicts of interest which have been felt to be irreconcilable. The paranoid style would thus appear to be a psychological device for projecting various symbols of evil on an opponent and for building emotional unity through a common sense of alarm and peril.

Since the phrase "paranoid style" is easily misinterpreted, it is well to take note of Hofstadter's own qualifications. He recognizes the obvious fact that the phenomenon has not been confined to America, although his examples suggest distinctive patterns of belief and emotion. If political styles can be examined in the manner of baroque or neo-classical artistic styles, then we might suspect that the American paranoid is at least as distinctive as the American Gothic.[2] Hofstadter also acknowledges that history has been filled with actual conspiracies of various sorts, and hence cautions that the paranoid style "has to do with the way in which ideas are believed and advocated rather than with the truth or falsity of their content." These words need elaboration if we are to avoid a fruitless debate over the reality of the Slave Power and abolitionist conspiracies. The first point to emphasize is that actual conspiracies from Aaron Burr to the American Communist Party have seldom been as significant social realities as the movements against alleged conspiratorial groups. We all know that the Civil War era was framed in 1859 and 1865 by two dramatic conspiracies; yet it should be obvious that the demented expectations of

John Brown and John Wilkes Booth were in no way so important as the collective fears and suspicions which gave meaning to Harpers Ferry and to Lincoln's assassination, and which drew on traditional images of abolitionist subversives and Slave Power plots. Similarly, while historians of the American Revolution have long dismissed the inflamed charges of pamphleteers as mere rhetoric, Bernard Bailyn has recently argued that the belief in British conspiracy was a vital element in Revolutionary ideology and in the definition of national identity.[3]

The truth or falsity of a given perception is often quite relative. When one is concerned with a complex social question such as the nature or existence of a conspiracy, there are so many variables and problems of definition that much depends on the observer's position, interests, and amount of information. Thus the belief in conspiracy can be treated as a theoretical construct, not necessarily less reasonable than other constructs which help explain disturbing and unexpected happenings. In retrospect we may see gross distortions in George Washington's conviction in 1774 that Parliament was acting on a deliberate, systematic plan to enslave the colonies, or in Abraham Lincoln's belief in 1858 that the Kansas-Nebraska Bill had been contrived with "an exactly fitted niche for the Dred Scott decision to afterward come in, and declare that perfect freedom of the people to be just no freedom at all." Yet these were not necessarily unreasonable interpretations of the information then available. Even the wildest theories of conspiracy must have some credibility to win the minds of judicious men. An explanatory framework which sharply polarized society into, let us say, the Power Elite and the deluded white collar workers, or the White Power structure and the exploited Blacks, may tell us as much about social realities as the image of a classless and conflict-free consensus. Moreover, as I hope to show later on, the imagery of counter-subversion may give symbolic expression to the deepest fears and needs of a people, and thus to truth of a most revealing kind.

The question of truth and falsity is related to the question of normality and abnormality. Hofstadter insists that while he means the term "paranoid style" to be pejorative, he does not use it in a clinical sense. Indeed, he writes that "it is the use of paranoid modes of expression by more or less normal people that makes the phenomenon significant." I agree, although I am more hesitant about making pejorative judgments or drawing sharp distinctions between normal and abnormal fantasies. The word "paranoid," as distinct from the disease of paranoia, may refer to patterns of behavior that can be found on a continuum from extreme abnormality to relative normality. And we all have our paranoid moments.

Let me emphasize that I have no intention of contributing to the great debate on the causes of the Civil War or of assigning causative weight to the paranoid style. I have no means of knowing how many Northerners believed in the Slave Power conspiracy, or with what sincerity or intensity. I have not sought to determine whether secession or the fighting morale of Southern troops can be explained by the belief that abolitionist subversives dominated the Republican Party. It is an indisputable though neglected fact that by the 1850's conspiratorial imagery had become a formalized staple in the political rhetoric of both North and South, appropriated by eminent statesmen and journalists as well as by fanatics. No doubt there are certain personality types in every society who always detect systematic intrigue behind the ordinary stumbling and inconsistent actions of political leaders. But in times of great internal conflict and uncertainty, such as the Civil War era or the 1960's, the line narrows between respectable ideology and what might normally be dismissed as the ravings of screwballs and nuts. The opinions of a John A. Stormer are significant not only because his first book, *None Dare Call It Treason,* has sold over seven million copies, but because his view that communism pervades the mass media, the universities, the churches, and the Eastern Establishment is only an extreme and rationalized form of widely diffused suspicions of modern secular culture.

Let me illustrate the importance of a patently abnormal fantasy by summarizing the argument of a book written soon after Lincoln's assassination, entitled *History of the Plots and Crimes of the Great Conspiracy to Overthrow Liberty in America.* The author, John Smith Dye, begins with the conventional Northern premise that slavery had been opposed by all the statesmen of the early Republic.[4]

Only when Calhoun rose to power were there dark signs of a Southern conspiracy that would not stop at murder to retain control over federal policy. When President Jackson defied Calhoun's heresy of states' rights, he narrowly escaped being shot by a man who was either hired or instigated by the Vice-President. Soon after Calhoun learned that President Harrison refused to cooperate in the plot to annex Texas, the President died of a mysterious illness, the symptoms closely resembling arsenic poisoning, and was succeeded by a Vice-President who had assured Calhoun of his support. If Tyler had been more pious, he might have been moved by the divine retribution which killed Calhoun's co-conspirators, Upshur and Gilmore, in the explosion on board the Princeton; yet in defiance of God's will, he named Calhoun to be Upshur's successor as Secretary of State. The Slave Power triumphed in annexing Texas and precipitating the Mexican War, only to discover that President Taylor opposed slavery in California and spurned Calhoun's request not to mention the Union in his annual message. It was inevitable, therefore, that Taylor should die like Harrison.

Since both Presidents Fillmore and Pierce were puppets of the Slave Power, there was a lull in political assassination. Pierce not only opened Kansas to slavery and plotted against Cuba, but compelled Justice Taney to keep the Dred Scott decision secret in order to assure the election of Buchanan, a Northern renegade who disguised his pro-slavery sentiments except when in the company of Southerners. Yet as President-elect the shifty Buchanan soon proved unreliable to the Slave Power, especially as he contemplated cabinet appointments. According to John Smith Dye, Buchanan dined at the National Hotel on February 23, 1857 (he had actually left Washington on February 3 for his country home in Pennsylvania). Since Northerners drink tea and Southerners coffee, agents of the Slave Power sprinkled arsenic in the bowls containing lump sugar for tea. Thus no Southern guest was harmed, though some sixty Northerners, including Buchanan, were severely poisoned, and thirty-eight died. (We might note at this point that during January and February, 1857, there were outbreaks of acute intestinal illness at various Washington hotels, including the National. Guests reported bad plumbing odors, and the board of health later blamed the illness on noxious sewer gas. On February 26 the New York *Herald* reported that the President-elect, then in Pennsylvania, had suffered the recurrence of an illness first contracted in Washington; but it did not interfere with his reception of visitors or his return to the Capital on March 2. By mid-March the press began reporting rumors of a poisoned rat in the watertank of the National Hotel and of an attempt by slaves to kill the President-elect.) [5] According to Dye, Buchanan was so intimidated by the assassination plot that he immediately became a tool of the Slave Power. Obviously Dye's account of the murderous crimes of the Slave Power seemed more credible in the light of Lincoln's assassination, and seemed to confirm his accusation that Lewis Payne and John H. Surratt had acted as the agents of Jefferson Davis.

We need not dwell on the obviously paranoid qualities of Dye's history of assassination, which has a curiously modern ring. The important point is that Dye simply fitted more details of personal evil into an explanatory framework that had been popularized by men like William H. Seward, Charles Sumner, and even Lincoln himself. The book can also be read as an explicit dramatization of the fairly conventional charge that the Slave Power—or slavery itself—had slowly poisoned the wellsprings of American life.

Dye's assumption that an era of unity and goodwill had preceded the emergence of a conspiratorial enemy is characteristic of much of the literature of counter-subversion. It is true that anti-conspiratorial movements often reinterpret history from the viewpoint of their own immediate crises, and try to assimilate earlier enemies to their own negative reference group. Robert Welch, for example, has identified the eighteenth-century Society of the Illuminati as an early form of communism which, because there was no John Birch Society to combat it, disseminated radical ideas in America after convulsing France in revolution.[6] But the belief that America would be united and pure if she had not been poisoned by a single great enemy necessarily obscures the interesting fact that Americans have perceived very different enemies in strikingly similar ways. It is in the responses to supposed subversion rather than in the threatening forces themselves that one finds the most interesting continuities.

Participants in the great slavery controversy were heirs

10

of an ideological tradition that had been shaped by Protestant fears of the Counter-Reformation, by English Whig interpretations of the Glorious Revolution, by the colonists' alarms over the plots of British ministers, and by Federalist hysteria over the French Revolution. As Bailyn has pointed out, Whig historiography had thoroughly familiarized American colonists with the idea that seemingly innocuous and unrelated acts of legislation might form parts of a systematic plan to subvert traditional liberties and concentrate power in the hands of an aristocratic oligarchy. We have seldom appreciated the significance of the popular conceptualization of the American Revolution. For if the nation's liberty and very existence had depended on the exposure of a conspiratorial plot to destroy traditional ways of life, one could reaffirm kinship with the Founding Fathers by reenacting the primal resistance to subversion. This may explain why so many Americans have instinctively equated liberty with suspicion, with being on guard, with grabbing up a musket when Paul Revere sounds an alarm through the night.

The image of British conspiracy in the American Revolution was in some ways a prototype for the later image of the Slave Power. Both were conceived as aristocratic oligarchies which, having seized the mechanisms of government, slowly undermined free constitutions and implemented systematic plans to enslave the people. On a different level of continuity, the Federalist image of French Illuminati foreshadowed later anti-abolitionist fantasies. Like the agents of the French Revolution, the abolitionists were supposedly the tools of a foreign power—in this case England; operating from secret cells, they deluded the public with subversive propaganda and plotted the destruction of religion, private property, and the family. Since both the Illuminati and abolitionists relied on the cunning manipulation of words to overthrow the social order, it was claimed they had forfeited the protection of civil liberties.

When we speak of prototypes and thematic continuities we should not lose sight of the concrete social and economic conflicts which sharply differentiated movements of counter-subversion. The paranoid style has been employed by many diverse groups for many purposes. Clearly the New England clergy who denounced Democratic-Republican societies shared little in common with later anti-abolitionists; there were very great differences between resisting the Boston Port Bill and the Fugitive Slave Law. The economic and status rivalries that gave rise to anti-Masonry should not be confused with the ethnic conflict that contributed to waves of anti-Catholicism, nor can either anti-Masonry or anti-Catholicism be homogenized with Jacksonian castigations of the Monster Bank. But one can acknowledge a wide range of differences in social contexts and political alignments and still identify a typology of American enemies. Indeed, one can easily interchange many paragraphs of anti-Masonic, anti-Catholic, and antislavery writing with only a few substitutions of words. Such similar modes of perceiving subversive enemies can be analyzed on two levels. First, it is possible that groups with quite different interests have been affected by common cultural needs and tensions, or have given expression, perhaps in distinctive forms, to widely diffused fears. We shall return to this aspect later on. The second level pertains to the historical transmission and appropriation of ideas.

There is still much to be learned about direct continuities between various movements of counter-subversion. We know it was the Anti-Masonic Party that first demonstrated the enormous political appeal of attacking a Monster Institution and demanding equal opportunity for all citizens. Though leading anti-Masons increasingly deflected their fire toward the supposed usurpations of President Jackson, the Jacksonian Democrats appropriated much of the anti-Masonic rhetoric against monopolistic privilege and a conspiratorial Monster Institution. In 1832 we find an "Anti-Conspirator" newspaper merging the causes of anti-Masonry and antislavery.[7] Various figures as prominent as Gerrit Smith and William H. Seward moved easily from denunciations of Freemasonry to denunciations of the Slave Power. Others, such as George Bourne and George Barrell Cheever, divided their talents between attacking slavery and the Catholic Church. It became commonplace in abolitionist literature to link the Slave Power with the Northern money power, which had first been delineated by Jacksonian publicists. We should not make too much of such connections, since there were many abolitionists, for example, who strongly opposed anti-Masonry and anti-Catholicism.

13

Moreover, each movement of counter-subversion sought to portray its own opponent as the only authentic and genuinely threatening enemy. Thus many abolitionists came to see the Know-Nothing movement as a Southern plot intended to divert the attention from the Slave Power to the relatively harmless Catholic Church. The important point is that by the late 1830's, when abolitionists lost faith in the policy of moral suasion, they could appropriate the inflamed phrases and rhetoric of a decade of anti-Masonic and anti-Catholic agitation, interlarded with Jacksonian allusions to a Monster Bank.

The external history of the Slave Power thesis can be briefly summarized, since most of the details have long been known. While a distinct image of the Slave Power did not appear until the late 1830's, its ingredients had been associated with earlier sectional conflict. Even in the eighteenth century, British reformers had stereotyped West India planters as petty tyrants corrupted by habits of unchecked power. In 1764 James Otis exploited this theme when he blamed the Sugar Act on a conspiracy of West India planters and merchants who had been morally perverted by slavery.[8] Thirty years later British writers supporting the West India interest dealt devastating blows to antislavery by linking the cause with Thomas Paine's supposed atheism and with the reign of terror in France and Santo Domingo. The lesson would not be lost on later foes of abolitionism. Although the New England clergy were equally horrified by the French Revolution, conservatives like Timothy Dwight also felt a deep an-

14

tipathy toward the Southern slave society, which seemed to stand in the way of converting the Republic into an empire of benevolence and godliness. Opposition to slavery's expansion was not quite the same as resistance to a Slave Power, and there were diverse motives behind Northern denunciations of the three-fifths ratio for apportioning political representation as well as Northern objections to the spread of slavery into Mississippi Territory and Louisiana. Yet Thomas Branagan voiced a complaint in 1805 that would become a battle cry in future decades: it was outrageous injustice, he wrote, for the "tyrants of the South" to gain political power over the citizens of the North by increasing the enslavement and oppression of the "exiled sons of Africa." At the very time when Northerners were nobly ridding themselves of the taint of slavery, the South was being rewarded for a villainy which disgraced all Americans alike.[9]

One should emphasize that as late as 1821 the minutes of the American Convention of Abolition Societies called for pragmatic plans that would not disrupt national unity, and warned against reproaching those "who by the conduct of their ancestors are placed in the condition of masters of slaves." During the explosive Missouri controversy of the two preceding years, Southern leaders denounced antislavery arguments as a hypocritical mask concealing a Federalist plot to dissolve the Union. Although Rufus King had opposed the Federalist secession movement during the War of 1812 and had a consistent record of resisting the expansion of slavery from the time

15

of the Northwest Ordinance, his leadership of antislavery forces in the Senate aroused the most hostile suspicions. Jefferson concluded that King was "ready to risk the Union for any chance of restoring his party to power and wriggling himself to the head of it"; Monroe thought that King aspired to lead a new confederation of New York and New England. The Missouri crisis evoked a temporary polarization that gave rise to imagery of subversion remarkably similar to that of later decades. In the South a sharpening of proslavery arguments was accompanied by growing fears of the political potency of antislavery. On November 16, 1819, an audience of some two thousand New Yorkers heard John T. Irving, the brother of Washington Irving, pose future alternatives of a "mighty empire of slaves" or an empire of men with constitutional as well as natural rights to life, liberty, and the pursuit of happiness.[10] Two years later Benjamin Lundy, the Quaker abolitionist, concluded that the Missouri Compromise had been a total victory for the South. Either the success and prosperity or the utter ruin of the Republic would now depend on the rising generation, to whom he dedicated his new *Genius of Universal Emancipation.* But though Lundy announced that either the Republic or the "hydra of iniquity" would have to be destroyed, the nation's political leaders had seen that when slavery was used as a symbol of political alignment, there could be an interaction of paranoid styles which would soon preclude compromise.[11]

Merton Dillon has recently portrayed Lundy as an important link between the political antislavery aroused by the Missouri crisis and the shift in the late 1830's toward political abolitionism.[12] Lundy's early experience in Missouri Territory not only convinced him that slavery could have been excluded from the area, but acquainted him with the first ventures to colonize Texas. As early as 1829 he warned of a Southern conspiracy to annex Texas as a means of multiplying slave states. His own extended visits to Texas in the early 1830's alerted him to plots to subvert the antislavery laws of the Mexican government and provided him with a framework for interpreting the Texas Revolution as part of a vast Southern conspiracy. Lundy's alarms over Texas coincided with a growing frustration among abolitionists as Northern mobs harassed lecturers, as the South sealed itself off from moral suasion, and as Congress turned its back on antislavery petitions. If Northern racial prejudice blunted the abolitionists' appeals to justice and humanity, Southern fears of slave insurrection brought a furious reaction to their ideology. During the summer of 1835, panic spread across large sections of the lower South after the capture of a Mississippi River pirate and slave stealer supposedly revealed the existence of a vast conspiratorial brotherhood which was vaguely associated with abolitionism because of its threat to slave property.[13] A wave of lynchings and murders, culminating in the shooting of Elijah P. Lovejoy at Alton, Illinois, convinced reformers like William Goodell that the evils of slavery went considerably beyond injustice to Negroes. By 1839 Goodell stated flatly that slavery was at war with the liberties of all Americans; even the Southern whites, subjected as they were to terrorism and mob violence, had become the slaves of slavery.[14] The Slave Power thesis was elaborated by men like Goodell, Gerrit Smith, Joshua Leavitt, and Alvan Stewart, and was linked with the rise of the Liberty Party following a failure to commit candidates of the major parties to antislavery principles. However, the thesis soon became common political currency as various groups of Northerners reacted to the annexation of Texas, the Mexican War, the controversies over the Wilmot Proviso and California, and the crisis over Kansas.

Again, we must emphasize the loose fit between the interests of concrete groups and a set of imagery appropriated by Liberty Leaguers, Conscience Whigs, Free Soilers, and Republicans. It was only in the 1850's and in response to the Compromise of 1850 and the Kansas-Nebraska Bill, that defensive rhetoric became transmuted into hardened conviction which required a reassessment of American history and a mobilization of sectional power. The events from 1850 to 1858, particularly the Fugitive Slave Law, the repeal of the Missouri Compromise, and the Dred Scott decision, suggested a degree of Southern unity, premeditation, and control which was hardly credible in earlier years; and this impression was reinforced when Southern radicals defended slavery as a positive good which was rightfully being protected by the federal government, and then demanded the reopening of the African trade and the annexation of Cuba. Conversely, the emergence of the Black Republicans and the appearance in Kansas of emigrant aid societies confirmed Southern fears that abolitionist conspirators had nearly gained control of the North and would not stop until they had seized the federal government. Without denying the importance of moderating pressures or of internal conflicts within each section, we can say with some confidence that earlier images of subversion took on sharper relief in the 1850's and became reified as two supremely menacing forces.

There were many complexities and variations, however, even in the definition of the Slave Power. Viewing the question from the eastern side of the Atlantic, *Blackwood's Magazine* defined the Slave Power in 1853 as "that control in and over the Government of the United States which is exercised by a comparatively small number of persons, distinguished from the other twenty millions of free citizens and bound together by a common interest by being the owners of slaves." At the beginning of the Civil War, the Irish economist John Elliot Cairnes explained the Slave Power as "that system of interests, industrial, social, and political, which has for the greater part of half a century directed the career of the American Union . . . [and which] constitutes the most formidable antagonist to civilized progress which has appeared for many centuries." [15] Such definitions were fairly commonplace in America, but they seldom indicated whether the Slave Power was confined to the wealthier planters, or whether it embraced all slave owners, including women, the executors of estates, and residents of border states; whether it was a purely political interest, as *Blackwood's* definition implied, or represented a total culture or civilization; and whether it included Northern business and political interests that supported Southern demands, as well as Southern politicians who had no personal ties with slavery.

Similar ambiguities arose concerning the strength and unity of the Slave Power. The 1853 *Blackwood's* article judged it "more absolute than that of any European aristocracy—almost as uncontrolled by public sentiment as that of an Asiatic potentate." Two years later, Charles Francis Adams conceded that the Slave Power, consisting of "three hundred and fifty thousand men, spreading over a large territorial surface, commanding the political resources of fifteen states," was also in undisputed possession of all "the official strongholds in the general government." [16] Speaking of the earlier move to annex Texas, George W. Allen saw the entire South moving "as one man, in an outbreak of frantic joy, at each indication of success, and venting the most outrageous passions whenever an adverse gust dashes across the path of their hope." [17] "They lay their mesmeric hands upon the moral pulse of the nation," complained George W. Julian, "and it ceases to beat. Nothing that is earthly can stand before the dread authority of these men. They are the reigning lords and *masters* of the people, white and black. Look at the facts." [18] Julian's phrenetic imagery and his blunt appeal to the facts could have been borrowed from any of a hundred anti-Masonic or anti-Catholic pamphlets. But like Freemasonry and Catholicism, the Slave Power represented a tiny minority whose strength was fragile if not illusory. Julian himself calculated that slaveholders constituted only 4 percent of the white population of the slave states, and 1 percent of the nation as a whole. Hated by millions of slaves who brooded over their wrongs, regarded with increasing hostility by the downtrodden poor whites, the slaveholders were also confronted, according to Julian, by the overwhelming power of public opinion throughout the civilized world. George M. Weston interpreted the aggressions of the Slave Power, particularly its efforts to acquire Cuba, as proof of its desperately weak situation. The South would never secede, he predicted in 1856, because slavery's only hope lay in expanding under the protection of the Federal Union.[19]

The image of the Slave Power conspiracy revealed still different contours when viewed from a non-abolitionist perspective. Many Northerners who had scorned abolitionism embraced the Slave Power thesis as an explanation for the Civil War. Thus in a speech at St. Louis in 1863, Charles D. Drake disavowed any sympathy for abolitionism but supported the Emancipation Proclamation as a justifiable blow against the treasons of the Slave Power: "When I strike at Slavery," he said, "it is because Slavery strikes at my country; and for that I would STRIKE IT DOWN!," an utterance which, we are told, brought "immense and prolonged applause." [20] John M. Botts, a Virginia Whig who served in Congress from 1839 to 1843, advanced the novel view that the Slave Power had no genuine interest in the institution of slavery. Demands for extending slavery had been a mere pretext for dividing and crushing the Whigs and thus expanding the power of the Democratic Party. Southern secessionists had early exploited the trick of branding opponents as Federalist secessionists and then as abolitionists. They had cunningly promoted Northern hysteria by insisting on the gag rule and by giving a proslavery interpretation to the Mexican War, which invited the Wilmot Proviso. By subtle design they had given birth to abolitionism, which they had then nursed and encouraged. After further arousing the country with blustering schemes to annex Cuba and Nicaragua, they had deliberately split the Democratic Party to ensure Lincoln's election and America's disunion.[21]

The charge that the Slave Power was linked with its opposite extreme of abolitionism seemed plausible to certain Northern Whigs and Southern Unionists. During the election of 1844 there were Whig accusations that James G. Birney, leader of the antislavery Liberty Party, had entered into a conspiracy with Democratic Party locofocos to ensure the triumph of Polk over Clay. In a wild book entitled *The Conspiracy Unveiled, the South Sacrificed*, written in 1863 by a Virginia Unionist, an assortment of negative groups congeal into a single conspiracy of locofoco Democrats, abolitionists, and Southern secessionists, whose lust for power is sacrificing the South to a

Negro oligarchy.[22] Of course the foes of Lincoln's administration took a different view, and sometimes perceived a conspiratorial alliance between abolitionists and what today would be termed the "military-industrial complex." Thus in 1863 the author of magazine articles entitled *The Washington Despotism* anticipated future left-wing rhetoric when he attacked "the shoddy aristocracy, army and navy contractors, and all that class that wax fat and wealthy as the country grows poor, and that count their gains by the prolongation of this war." He sounded another theme which has also pervaded American thought, more commonly associated with reactionary causes: the dictators in Washington, he wrote, were bent on "the complete prostration of the country, so as to render it an easy prey to the diplomacy and intrigue of European statesmen." [23]

We should not dismiss these conflicting versions of the paranoid style as self-negating aberrations. The idea of conspiracy was a symbolic means of accounting for the subtle truth that abolitionists and Southern secessionists often played mutually supporting roles and seemed to be staging a premeditated performance to a bewildered and powerless audience. Conspiracy was also a way of explaining the paradox that the humanitarian war aim of emancipation required an uncompromising war effort sustained by profit-seeking businessmen. The issue of slavery, though responded to in many diverse ways, gave a coherence and sharper focus to perceptions only dimly adumbrated in other movements of counter-subversion.

23

I suggested earlier that the various images of subversion in the antebellum era might have given expression to common cultural needs and tensions. I should now like to offer a general hypothesis that provides a way, though by no means the only way, of conceptualizing the social dynamics of conspiratorial thought. In a recent article on "Status Anxiety and American Reform," Robert W. Doherty calls attention to the theoretical gaps in the now familiar thesis that a disposition toward reform sprang from status anxiety induced by rapid upward and downward mobility. Doherty proposes the concepts of role-playing and reference group behavior as intervening variables between mobility, anxiety, and social action. He advises us to look more closely at how reformers' perceptions of themselves and of opponents underpinned self-evaluation and action.[24]

If we interpret the language of antebellum writers as symbolic action, representing a meaningful response to perceived situations, we find added encouragement for thinking in terms of roles and performances. Numerous participants in the slavery controversy, without sensing the full implications of their choice of words, adopted the imagery of the stage. Thus Texas is to be a "new Theatre" for the slavery agitation; by 1839 abolitionists have abandoned comedy for "the more grave enactment of a tragedy"; "new scenes" are always being acted out, and conspirators have "played the game of blood too often."

These random illustrations acquire more significance

in the light of Erving Goffman's remarkable book, *The Presentation of Self in Everyday Life.* Goffman offers theoretical models that deal with the attempts we make to define situations, to sustain impressions, and thus to control the impressions others receive. After observing that any social performance presents an idealized view of a given situation, Goffman quotes Charles H. Cooley to the effect that each profession or class has a cant or pose which its members unconsciously assume "but which has the effect of a conspiracy to work upon the credulity of the rest of the world." [25] Taking this as his cue, Goffman defines a team as a set of individuals "whose intimate cooperation is required if a given projected definition of the situation is to be maintained." It follows that if a performance is to be effective, whether the team consists of rebellious schoolgirls or salesmen in a store conning a customer, the extent and nature of cooperation must be concealed backstage. "A team," Goffman concludes, "has something of the character of a secret society." He adds that since "we all participate on teams we must all carry within ourselves something of the sweet guilt of conspirators," concealing or playing down certain facts in order to maintain a given impression.[26] Sometimes a team performance has the character of an official ceremony, reinforcing the moral values of the community. Yet "every role has its defrocked priests to tell us what goes on in the monastery, and the press has always shown a lively interest in these confessions and exposés." [27] To the historian these words immediately recall the apostate Free-

25

masons, Catholics, and Mormons, as well as the Southerners converted to antislavery, who revealed backstage truth to counter-conspirators.

But how does this highly generalized theory of personal interaction apply to the use of paranoid styles in the slavery controversy? The answer lies, I think, in evidence of a sharp increase in confusion over social roles during the antebellum decades. Without making exaggerated claims for the uniqueness of the so-called Middle Period, it was clearly a time of unprecedented fluidity and growth, stimulated in part by the transportation revolution. No doubt there was a certain changeability in roles even in the most stable New England towns and Virginia counties. Yet men who moved to booming cities or newly-created communities encountered a shifting mélange of teams and alliances. Individual success depended, in large measure, on effective presentations of self and on convincing definitions of new situations. But there were few indigenous models for the man of wealth, the man of culture, or even the philanthropist. The educational mechanisms were ill-suited to prepare men for the variety of new roles they would have to play. New statuses and relationships, whether economic, religious, or political, demanded innovations in staging. And this was, we should recall, the great era of political rallies and religious revivals. Mobility could also lead to a kind of subjective frustration which Goffman has shrewdly analyzed. Even when an individual is successful in acquiring a coveted status, he often finds that his new position is

26

as insecure as his former one, that he had naively believed in the performances put on by his elders of the prestigious rank, and that he must now stage a similar show.[28] We may conclude, therefore, that rapid mobility often makes men self-consciously aware of aspects of role-playing which are taken for granted in tradition oriented societies.

There is considerable evidence of concern over such matters during the quarter-century preceding the Civil War. Both on the popular and literary levels of culture, we find a virtual obsession with hoaxes, imposters, frauds, confidence men, and double identities. Such themes are commonplace, for example, in the works of Hawthorne and Melville, and are taken up with a morbid intensity by Twain, who remains our most revealing commentator on antebellum culture. An excellent illustration of the extent of role confusion as well as despair over public credulity can be found in David Meredith Reese's *Humbugs of New York*, which appeared in 1838. Reese, a down-to-earth physician, was disturbed by the gullibility of an urban population which swallowed a journalistic moon hoax, lionized phrenologists and animal magnetists, spent fortunes on medical quackery, and believed the lurid and fabricated disclosures of Maria Monk, who had supposedly escaped from a Canadian nunnery. In Reese's eyes it was no wonder that the public, having been hoodwinked by an itinerant troupe of charlatans and imposters, should now fall prey to ultra-Abolitionism, ultra-temperance, and ultra-Protestantism, including the absurd sham of Mormonism. Yet, as the founder of Mormonism had earlier said, when faced with the confusing claims of Presbyterians, Baptists, and Methodists, "In the midst of this war of words, and tumult of opinion . . . What is to be done? Who, of all these parties, are right? or, are they all wrong together? If any one of them be right, which is it? and how shall I know it?" [29] The central question in Joseph Smith's dilemma was credibility of performance.

It was hardly accidental, therefore, that the romantic ideal, in politics as well as art, was the man who wears no mask, who plays no role, whose appearance and behavior are at one with his inner self. In a society increasingly aware of role-playing and backstage secrets, as a result of the disruptions and discontinuities of accelerated mobility, there was clearly a yearning for authenticity, spontaneity, and naturalness. From Jefferson to Emerson, Hawthorne, and Melville, writers saw the city not simply as an abode of evil, but as a place of contrived and ambiguous performances. One suspects that many of the protests against the heartlessness of a competitive, free-for-all society were far less concerned with social injustice than with the way the acquisitive spirit debased and commercialized social roles. This was, after all, one of the meanings of depersonalization and dehumanization. Even the simplicity and spontaneity of the man of nature soon became stylized in staged performances which ranged in credibility from Andrew Jackson to Davy Crockett, from Henry David Thoreau to Joaquin Miller. In the era of P. T. Barnum, whom could you trust? How could you keep from being taken in? The freedom which allowed each citizen to go his own way in life, to become a self-made man, also opened the way to mass deception. A more secure people would presumably have been less responsive to the central theme of the American paranoid style: namely, that just when you think you're making out, you're really being had! There are many indications that the image of an expansive, subversive force was a means of articulating individual and communal anxieties over being duped and slipping behind.

Various interest groups in America had long sought to portray their opponents as confidence men whose cloak of goodwill concealed an insidious scheme to rob the public. To contrast one's own openness and sincerity of motives with the secrecy and artifice of an antagonist was partly a matter of tactics and partly a cultural ritual reaffirming democratic values. The counter-subversive could achieve at least temporary escape from the uncertainties of role-playing by joining in an ostensibly authentic crusade against a symbol of duplicity. And such crusades were inevitably self-confirming, since any collective response of the opponent could be interpreted as proof of his collusive solidarity. As we have already seen, the basic pattern was set by the ideology of the American Revolution, which supposedly exposed the backstage designs of the British government. This initial pattern acquired new and fuller dimensions as Federalists exposed an international revolutionary conspiracy, as Republicans seized upon the Hartford convention as a symbol of dark treason, and as anti-Masonry, anti-Catholicism, and

Jackson's anti-Bank crusade alerted the public to an increasing number of subversive forces. Because the tactic was adopted by so many groups and played upon the personal anxieties of so many people, it contributed to a growing fear of the discrepancy between appearance and reality.

It was within this setting that Garrisonian abolitionists launched their campaign to bring the nation to repentance, and to shame the South into freeing the slaves. This moralistic approach struck at the heart of national accommodations that had long defined slavery as a necessary and therefore tolerable evil. It also challenged the more positive rationalizations for slavery that had begun to appear in the South. Throughout the nation, but particularly in the slaveholding areas, it was essential to prove that abolitionists were not the selfless humanitarians they pretended to be, but rather irresponsible fanatics who were being used by the British to confuse and divide the gullible public. Whereas the unsettled state of opinion in the North was dangerously susceptible to fraudulent performances, the South still enjoyed the blessing of natural and unaffected relationships. Much of the appeal of the cavalier mythology, which was largely Northern in origin, lay in its portrayal of Southern social roles as a true expression of natural realities.

But when abolitionists hit upon the image of a Slave Power conspiracy, they had found a powerful symbol that could stand for all the contradictions between appearance and reality in American society. The discrepancy between the image of benign plantation life and the backstage brutalities of slavery dwarfed and absorbed all other deceptions. It was out of subservience to the Slave Power that Northern businessmen, politicians, and clergymen had become masters at double-dealing. If the image of abolitionist subversives helped to silence dissent and preserve traditional definitions which had repressed the objective contradictions of American slavery, the image of the Slave Power provided a means of conceptualizing and attacking all the threatening illusions of American life.

2

Polarization:
The Abolitionists as Subversives;
The Slave System Impregnable
to the Word of Truth

Slave masters have generally lived with a shadowy dread of insurrection, even when unchallenged by abolitionist attacks. Such fear, while leading often to paranoid suspiciousness, was a realistic response to genuine danger. It may also have reflected the insecurity of an authoritarian role often recently acquired and lacking in traditional sanctions. For whatever reasons, there were structural elements in the master-slave relationship which made slaveholders of quite different nationalities acutely sensitive to any external force that might conceivably trigger a slave revolt. In the eighteenth century, Caribbean planters shared a common fear that in wartime foreign enemies would exploit their vulnerability; they shared similar suspicions that heterodox religious ideas would incite blacks to violence. And when antislavery societies emerged in the 1780's, French and British planters responded with similar assumptions and strategies.

32

There was nothing unusual or distinctive, then, about Virginia's alarm in 1775 over Lord Dunmore's offer of freedom to escaped slaves (Cuba, for example, had frequently employed the same tactic against Jamaica); or about the furious denunciations of Quakers in 1790 by Southern congressmen; or about forensic attempts to define slavery as too incendiary a topic for legislative debate. Defenders of British West India slavery created an image of abolitionist subversion which anticipated most of the themes I am about to discuss.

Yet by virtue of the American Revolution, Southern slaveholders occupied an extraordinary position which inevitably influenced their response to the abolitionist challenge. The political leverage of West India proprietors might increase or decrease with their economic fortunes, but only in America was there a fixed and direct tie between slave ownership and political power. Only in America did slaveholders play a central role in establishing a nation and creating representative institutions. West India legislators sometimes threatened secession, but they could not appeal to a body of common revolutionary theory justifying secession in the defense of property, or point to a compact they had helped frame, arguing that its very being rested on an understood agreement not to "intermeddle with slavery." Representatives of the Caribbean interest might denounce British abolitionists as dangerous fanatics employed by the French, but they retained a certain deference toward parliamentary leaders who echoed the very words of abolitionist pamphlets.

In America this would have been inconceivable, and of course there were no Pitts, Wilberforces, or Romillys to give antislavery an aura of aristocratic prestige; nor were Southern slaveholders dependent for patronage on party leaders like Pitt, who could afford to contribute eloquent rhetoric, if little else, to the antislavery cause. Not only could Southern politicians excoriate any public figure who showed sympathy for abolitionism, but they could rely on Northern newspaper editors to do the main work of isolating agitators and putting them in their place.[1] The image of the abolitionist as subversive was not a distinctively Southern phenomenon, although Southern interests and demands were very much in the minds of Northern defenders of the status quo.

A final difference between the United States and other slaveholding areas can be seen in the interaction of paranoid styles. The idea of a British Slave Power conspiracy could never have been credible, at least after American independence, and British planters never had the need to respond to such a charge. Indeed, their morale and aspirations would probably have been raised by being taken so seriously. But in America the Slave Power image was ultimately matched by the image of John Brown as the destroying angel of Black Republicanism. It should be stressed that these opposing symbols were intimately related, both through symbiotic evolution and through the historical associations attached to despotic power, subversion, and martyrdom.

John Brown's raid was a perfect fulfillment of the old

prophecy that abolitionists, despite their professions of nonviolence, really aimed at inciting slaves to insurrection. As far back as the 1780's, spokesmen for the British Caribbean interest warned that agitating for a bill to reform even the worst abuses of the slave trade would encourage slave unrest by giving blacks the impression they had friends in high places. A few years later, conservatives in various countries immediately attributed the great slave revolt in Santo Domingo to the undercover agents and inflammatory propaganda of the *Amis des Noirs*, who were seen in France as saboteurs employed by Britain, much as British abolitionists were charged with being the tools of French Jacobinism. The myth that abolitionists were directly responsible for the bloodbath of Santo Domingo became an entrenched part of master class ideology, in Latin America as well as the United States. It gave substance to the argument of clear and present danger, and thus served as an excuse for suppressing even the slightest criticism of slavery. It also gave expression to fears of being infiltrated, of being secretly penetrated, seized and overthrown at one's most vulnerable point. It was no accident that abolitionists were sometimes likened to witches and demons, or that New Englanders were continually reminded of their history of mysticism and fanaticism, dating back to the Salem trials. "The efforts of these conspirators," we are informed, "at their midnight meetings, where the bubbling cauldron of abolition was fulfilled with its pestilential materials, and the fire beneath kindled by the breath of the fanatics, has reminded us of the witch scene in MacBeth." [2] If the mass of Southern blacks could stand imaginatively for the sinful passional instincts deep in the bowels of Southern life, the slave states had to guard their collective soul from being secretly seized from within and possessed.

For some twenty years following the Santo Domingo explosion, the South's fear of insurrection centered on subversive influences from outside the United States. Attempts to exclude West India Negroes, whether slave or free, suggest the familiar nativist pattern of associating internal danger with diabolical alien forces. No doubt the intense nationalism of the early years of the Republic reinforced this tendency to link slave unrest with foreign troublemakers. While some critics insisted that white conspirators stood behind each slave plot that was uncovered, the charge was difficult to sustain without even specious evidence.[3] In this respect it was embarrassing that all the major slave plots antedated the rise of militant abolitionism.

We have already mentioned the hysteria evoked in 1835 by the exposure of a supposed criminal conspiracy, described by a New Orleans City Council report as "the most bloody and extensive scheme of devastation, massacre and ruin, which the human heart has ever conceived." [4] But while John A. Murrell's secret brotherhood had allegedly plotted a slave insurrection for private gain, the membership was Southern and there were only the vaguest intimations of abolitionist complicity. Even in the 1840's and 1850's, when there were more direct warnings of abolitionist agents infiltrating the South, usually cloaked as clergymen, one senses that the culprits were simply moderates who failed to meet the tests of proslavery zeal. In describing "the consequences of abolition agitation," in 1857, Edmund Ruffin spoke of "the many abolition agents, male and female, lay and clerical, who, in various ostensible business employments, have long been operating on our slaves, often under the hospitable shelter of our own roofs, and as our pretended friends." [5] But this detection of supposed abolition agents sounds like an attempt at ideological discipline within the Southern community. The ostensibly loyal citizens Ruffin had in mind were the counterparts to twentieth-century liberals accused of covert communism.

Since the fear of imprisonment or lynching apparently deterred abolitionist subversives from carrying out their worst designs, Southern critics concentrated on what they termed the "calculated effects" of inflammatory propaganda. Again and again they referred to incendiary pamphlets "calculated to excite the negroes of the Southern States to rise and massacre their masters." [6] Abolition, Calhoun announced in 1836, was no longer in the hands of "quiet and peaceful, but I cannot add harmless Quakers. It is now under the control of ferocious zealots." Accordingly, the states had a right to legislate against "publications calculated to excite insurrection." [7] In the same year William Drayton mourned over the evil times that had arrived when Americans had no scruples about tearing off "the seals which our Fathers set upon the question

37

of slavery." The abolitionists were determined "to break up the foundations of the great deep of public order—to throw the whole organization of southern society into chaos—light the torch of rapine and whet the knife of murder." It was essential to get the facts about slavery before the public. Any American, Drayton added, "who can, without alarm, witness the development of the *abolition conspiracy*, would scarcely be roused by the 'crack of doom.' " [8] Calhoun was alarmed enough to argue that unless Congress passed a law to stop the mailing of such literature, officials of the postal service would in effect be the agents and abettors of the conspiracy.[9] Demanding that Northern states pass laws suppressing antislavery publications, Governor George McDuffie of South Carolina reminded his own legislature of the fearful consequences of "*amis des noires* philanthropy," which had also had a "small and contemptible beginning." In his own judgment, "the laws of every community should punish this species of interference with death, without benefit of clergy." [10]

Northern resistance to the Fugitive Slave Law aroused nightmare images of vast organizations of slave stealers who would drain the South of wealth.[11] Even more threatening, however, were the nests of abolitionists planted in Kansas for the obvious purpose of subverting the institution in Missouri, Arkansas, and Texas. It is highly significant that many Southerners saw the Kansas struggle as an abolitionist attempt to win a base for infiltrating the more recently settled slave states, while Free Soilers perceived it as proof of the Slave Power's imperial expansion. Voicing a Southern version of the domino theory, John Townsend warned that the loss of Kansas would inevitably lead to the loss of Missouri. From such a base, underground railroads "might diverge to every city, town, and plantation," leading to insurrection and a "war of extermination." Townsend's apprehensions seemed confirmed by events in Texas. Just prior to the election of 1860, Texas newspapers exposed an abolition plot "to poison as many people as they could on Sunday, and on the day of election to burn the houses and kill as many of the women and children as they could while the men were gone to the election." These crimes, to be executed by Negroes and Kansas outlaws, had clearly been planned outside Texas. One of Townsend's Fort Worth correspondents reported that the majority of Texans "believe that Lincoln is the head and representative of this *Abolition Aid Society*, which sent John Brown to Virginia, and which is now giving us so much trouble here." [12] One is struck by the thought that this letter writer may now have great-grandchildren who express rather similar fears.

The contest over Kansas solidified the picture of antislavery as a revolutionary force working for the violent overthrow of constitutional government. In the 1830's the American Antislavery Society had been branded as a seditious, unconstitutional organization, but this vague accusation was based on the anachronistic premise that it was illegal for private pressure groups to "usurp" the functions of government by agitating political questions.[13] The Kansas struggle made it easier to assimilate abolitionism with concepts of conspiratorial violence, as personified earlier by Jacobins, Illuminati, and Freemasons. Thus it was claimed that immediately after the passage of the Kansas-Nebraska Bill, the Black Republicans in Congress plotted to expel all slaveholders from Kansas at whatever cost. Members of the Kansas Aid Society took a fearful oath, reminiscent of the alleged oaths of Illuminati and Freemasons, that they would violate any law and sacrifice their lives if necessary in order to uphold the free soil principles of the organization. By 1856 several turncoats had revealed the plans of secret military organizations, the so-called Sharpe's-rifle Christians, who had not only shed innocent blood for political effect but now conspired to drive the North and South into civil war. In the words of one newspaper, "the Black Republicans intend to Dissolve the Union . . . . They have proceeded in a regular gradation of acts, beginning at an early day, to prepare everything, to have each man placed in a suitable position, in which he was to play his part, and having the party thoroughly drilled for the final accomplishment of their conspiracy." [14] Congressman William Russell Smith of Alabama noted that the treason of the emigrant aid societies was "dark and hidden and sly." People complained of the brutality of the so-called "border ruffians" from Missouri, but at least there was a manly openness to their violence. "There is more devil in a sneak," Smith said, "than in a bully." [15]

The description of abolitionists as sneaks fitted in with a more generalized conception of Yankees as shifty, cowardly hypocrites who concealed their aggressive designs behind a mask of pious benevolence. A writer in the *Southern Quarterly Review* argued that the South had less to fear from the more extreme, outspoken abolitionists than from Northern journalists and reviewers who, fearing the label of abolitionist, attacked slavery by subtle innuendo. Echoing similar sentiments, and anticipating a major theme of anti-communism, Clement C. Clay proclaimed that "an army with banners is preferable to a Trojan Horse." The supposedly moderate free soil measures restricting the expansion of slavery were simply a cloak for total abolition.[16]

We do not ordinarily think of proslavery writers attacking the principles of secrecy and exclusiveness, or maintaining, as Robert Toombs did in 1855, that "publicity is the lifeblood of a representative Republic." Yet proslavery writers were no less eager than abolitionists to uncover the discrepancies between appearance and reality. Opponents of Masonry and the money power had concentrated their fire on the evils of monopoly and exclusiveness. For Toombs, free soil meant the exclusion of slaveholders from the common territories, which was nothing less than an act of aggression toward fifteen states.[17] The sudden rise of the Know-Nothing Party could be interpreted as proof of the trends toward secrecy and exclusiveness in the North. Thus Toombs claimed that Massachusetts Know-Nothings had allied with abolitionists in an attempt to nullify the rational compromises that had settled the slavery issue. Whereas the South, according to B. F. Stringfellow, extended a welcoming hand to all immigrants, secret nativist societies connived in the North for a repeal of the naturalization laws. That the demon of secrecy pervaded the North could be seen in the proliferation of trade unions and strange fraternal societies, largely made up of propertyless citizens. What tied the Know-Nothing and secret society movements to abolitionism was a common interest in expropriating private property and in dissolving the Whig Party.[18]

The idea of undercover organizations also explained the North's addiction to criminal disorder and political corruption. In the eyes of Jabez Curry of Alabama, abolition was part of a general spirit of "mobocratic misrule and plunder," manifested in Millerism, Mormonism, spirit-rappings, and socialism: "Secret watchwords pass readily from mouth to mouth; organized bands wait but for an occasion to despoil and divide; burglaries and garroting and assassinations fill the columns of the newspapers." A writer on "Abolition and Sectarian Mobs" argued that the prevalence in the North of urban violence and lawlessness was not the result of "sudden or temporary excitement," but of "extensive organizations, founded on . . . permanent opposition to the Constitution and laws of the country." The abolitionist banner had been appropriated by a group of totally amoral office seekers who had risen to power through a series of corrupt coalitions and disgraceful bargains, and who promoted domestic disorder to advance their private ambitions.[19]

These themes were often spliced into the Jacksonian scenario of the history of American parties. Thus abolitionists had supposedly played a part in Federalist conspiracies against the administrations of Jefferson and Madison. As the ideological descendants of Hamilton, or of Tories who opposed the Revolution, they had generally resisted the liberal measures which expressed the will of the people. Their monarchical leanings were exposed by their subservience to British standards and British opinion. John Quincy Adams, whose pretended conversion to democracy proved to be a fraud, had served as a link between the defeats of American monarchism and a new British-Federalist plot to plunder the South. When these royalists expressed a maudlin concern for the African, it was only a mask to conceal their goal of enslaving the white man. According to A. P. Butler of South Carolina, it was Virginia who had played the historical role of King Lear, freely bestowing her northwestern domains to the American people; Butler left it to his audience to decide which sections had played the parts of Cordelia and ungrateful Regan.[20]

There were a number of incidents in the 1830's which gave some credibility to the common charge that abolitionists were the dupes and tools of British aggression. Garrison's publicized first visit to England coincided with the last, triumphant stage of British abolition. American critics pounced upon his remarks disparaging his native land, and indignantly quoted the demands of British orators for universal emancipation, which were interpreted much like later Russian demands for worldwide socialism. George Thompson's tumultuous visit to America confirmed the picture of perfidious Albion sending or employing spies "to foment discord among our people, array brother against brother . . . to excite treasonable opposition to our government; to preach hatred and hostility against our sacred Union; to excite our slave population to rise and butcher their masters; to render the South a desert, and the country at large the scene of fraternal war." This writer continued, "England had wronged us heretofore, but it was as an open foe; and as an open and honorable foe was she met and chastised. But the amount of former wrongs—even those which have reddened land and sea with the blood of our people —is trifling compared with the injuries contemplated in this interference." [21]

It is interesting to note that Brazilian slaveholders were similarly convinced that England employed philanthropy as a cunning pretext for economic imperialism. Britain's long campaign to suppress the slave trade to Brazil, often by blatantly coercive measures, raised legitimate suspicions that antislavery was being used as an excuse for policing the high seas, for reducing the productivity of competing sugar growers, and for gaining control over foreign markets. In America, Britain's increasing adoption of antislavery policies was sometimes seen as a means of promoting the cotton producing interests of the East India Company. Duff Green charged that England had found two principal modes of maintaining her economic ascendancy: "One is by repeal of their corn laws . . . ; the other is by destroying slavery—to render it impossible for other manufacturing states to obtain the raw material as cheaply as through her." In the 1860's he surmised that the antislavery conspiracy was part of an elaborate imperialistic scheme that included the Grand Trunk Railroad of Canada, the British naval depot on Puget Sound, and French designs on Mexico.[22]

Unlike the Brazilians, who still depended on a continuing labor supply from Africa, Americans were usually willing to praise the motives which had led Britain to outlaw the slave trade. Thus a writer in the *Southern Literary Messenger* conceded that Wilberforce and his associates were "as pure philanthropists as the world ever saw." Yet there were men in the British government who had converted "this noble and generous feeling of the *people* at large" into an instrument "of national aggrandizement, and . . . a cloak for their designs upon America." It was easier to respect the motives of a Wilberforce or Clarkson because they had concentrated their efforts against the African trade, expecting gradual emancipation to follow the closing off of fresh labor supplies. But American writers also took satisfaction in observing that England had disregarded the inhumanity of the slave trade so long as the trade had promoted her national interests. She had bequeathed an onerous burden to her former colonists who were now forced to accept an institution for which they were not responsible. Calvin Colton expressed a comforting and widespread view when he defined both slavery and abolition as "foreign evils." [23]

The Texas controversy gave proslavery leaders an ideal opportunity to dramatize the connection between antislavery and British imperialism. There is no reason for us to review the well-known history of annexation. The relevant point is that men like Calhoun and Duff Green strengthened their demand for immediate annexation by revealing an alleged British conspiracy, aided by abolitionist subversives, to create a free soil satellite on America's southwestern border. The specter of a foreign antislavery bastion west of Louisiana was, in Thomas Hart Benton's phrase, "a clap of thunder in a clear sky." [24]

Undeterred by their failure in Texas, the abolitionists and their aristocratic mentors continued to wage war on slavery as the first step toward overthrowing republican government. The periodical press proved to be England's great "wedge" for splitting the American people in two. Magazines like *Blackwood's* disseminated abolitionist myths among the Whig mercantile community, which by tradition and temperament was disposed toward disloyalty and a fawning deference to British opinion. It is significant that so many proslavery writers implied that there would be no difficulty in disposing of native abolitionists if it were not for the support they received from a foreign power. There are striking parallels between later Populist fantasies of British goldbugs who dominated the American economy and proslavery accusations that British gold financed the abolitionist movement, the underground railroad, and the treasonous machinations of Joshua Giddings, Charles Sumner, and other backers of General Frémont. England, like the modern Soviet Union, appeared to be the fomenter of all America's troubles.[25]

Although abolitionism was associated, as we have seen, with Federalism and aristocracy, it was also conceived as a revolutionary force that threatened the basic values and institutions of society. This apparent contradiction is less puzzling when we recall that the heirs of liberal revolutions have commonly interpreted radical challenges to the social order, particularly to private property, as counter-revolutions instigated by those who had originally been dispossessed of power. Thus the same critics could identify abolitionism with the old conservative foes of the past, and also link it with the new heresies of Fourierism, "freeloveism," Mormonism, socialism, and communism. The main point was that abolitionism was never what it seemed to be. Its adherents shouted for the Union when they really aimed at destroying the Union. They used sanctimonious words and practiced atheism. The key to the true character of abolitionism—as indeed to later subversive foes—was supposed to lie in its inherent tendency to disintegrate respect for law, property, and religion. Thus the bloodshed in Kansas, to say nothing of Harpers Ferry, proved that the ideas and principles of the Republican Party led directly to the overthrow of constitutional government by force and violence.[26]

As early as 1850 Senator Robert Mercer Hunter of Vir-

47

ginia warned that an antislavery faction, by no means small in numbers, was seeking "to convert this Government . . . into an instrument of warfare upon the institution of Slavery in the States." Nine years later Sydenham Moore, a congressman from Alabama, pointed out that the American political system contained no safeguards which could prevent a fanatical, revolutionary party from seizing unchecked power by deluding and manipulating a sufficient number of voters. During the intervening years, numerous writers expressed alarm over the cankering infection or plague which was contaminating Northern opinion. In 1863 the author of a series of newspaper articles on "the great Northern plague" concluded that the war might be a blessing in disguise if only the country's moral and political atmosphere could be purified by sweeping away all the infected bodies of abolitionists. The trouble was that the war was not reducing the number of abolitionists, since they remained safe at home in their easy chairs. By dwelling on the metaphor of contagious infection, these counter-subversives gave expression to a more generalized anxiety over the gullibility of the public and the difficulty of predicting or controlling shifts of opinion.[27]

As writers employed the imagery of disease and evil spirits, metaphor often blurred into paranoid explanation. The charge that "cunning and malign spirits" were infecting innocent multitudes with abolitionism may have been merely figurative language. But in a remarkable book of 1863 entitled *Interior Causes of the War: The*

Nation Demonized and its President a Spirit-Rapper, we find such figures of speech transformed into the underlying causes of sectional conflict.[28] The anonymous author of this work maintained that it was no coincidence that the fad of spiritualism had crazed the North for a dozen years preceding the war, or that spirit-rapping had been embraced by men like Salmon Chase, Joshua Giddings, Horace Greeley, and Henry Ward Beecher, to say nothing of numerous abolitionists. Lincoln himself was "a spiritualist of the abolition school." Far from regarding spirit rappings as a hoax, this alarmist charged that the country had fallen into the hands of men who were "demonically magnetized," and who determined a "death-dealing policy" dictated by malign spirits. We are told that even General George McClellan was "rapped into command," a conclusion which Lincoln might well have been persuaded to accept! But however eccentric this writer may have been, he was hardly unique in his view of abolitionism as a manifestation of evil spirits which had corrupted the churches and prepared the public mind for self-destructive war. We need only recall the recent efforts to levitate and exorcise the Pentagon by modern hippie spiritualists to appreciate the persistent appeal and social significance of demonology.

Before turning to the abolitionist version of demonology, we should summarize the implications of the proslavery paranoid style. By the 1840's, American slaveholders had become increasingly aware of the discrepancy between their own self-image and the way they

49

were perceived by the outside world. Far more than most counter-subversives, the defenders of slavery had tangible interests at stake which were threatened by the major trends of Western history. In 1842 a writer in the *Southern Quarterly Review* scoffed at attempts to intimidate slaveholders with such "hobgoblins" as the "world's voice" and the "world's opinion." If there was truth to the claims of the periodical press, then the South "will take its ground against the world and . . . will obtain the victory in the contest." [29] This mood of embattled defiance could lead to paranoid suspicions and repressions much like those exhibited by modern South Africa.

We may conclude that the image of abolitionist subversion was a means of shoring up communal values, and of arriving at a sharper regional—and hopefully national—self-definition. It provided a test of Northern sincerity and goodwill, since it forced Northern leaders either to join in suppressing a common foe or to reveal their covert sympathy for an un-American force. To borrow again from Erving Goffman's terminology, Southern slaveholders and their Northern allies cooperated in a team performance which imposed a special interpretation on the growing dissonance between chattel slavery and liberal ideology. The interpretation required that certain aspects of American slavery be concealed backstage and also that critics of the institution be defined as wild fanatics or scheming imposters. Antislavery was seldom conceived of as a monolithic power, analogous to Freemasonry or the Catholic Church. The image of the abolitionist conspirator was more akin to the later image of the anarchist or internationalist Jew. Essentially weak and cowardly, he would pose no threat in a fair and open fight. But by slyly manipulating words, controlling popular media, and infiltrating institutions, he could enlist an army of fellow travelers. No image could better express the sense of being isolated by bewildering shifts in cultural styles and ideology, or the frustrations of an essentially rural, mechanically oriented society when confronted by the verbal sophistication of the urban world.

The enemies of slavery, for their part, were in the difficult strategic position of attacking an established institution. Defenders of the established order have always had the advantage of interpreting a blow against any particular institution as a blow against law, government, the family, and true religion. On the other hand, the very concept of slavery was freighted with philosophical and historical associations which added emotional resonance to the abolitionist cause.[30] Western literature, sacred as well as secular, pictured slavery as a terrifying and unmerited fate, from the bondage in Egypt of Old Testament Israelites to the captivity of innocent Christians by Barbary pirates. Both in literal and metaphorical usage, slavery was a symbol of exploitation, of total dependence, of the surrender of will and individuality. In the eyes of most Americans, Europeans had long been the docile slaves of tyrannical kings and lords, just as Roman Catholics, in the eyes of Protestants, were the spiritual slaves of their church. Moreover, as we have already noted, American patriots of the Revolutionary era were convinced that the king's ministers were pursuing a systematic plot to enslave the colonists. Enslavement of the American people was the supposed objective of the Illuminati, of the French Directory, of the Anglophile Federalists, of the Freemasons, and of the Catholic Church. In the rhetoric of the paranoid style, slavery has always been the inevitable fate of any people who fail to heed alarms and unite against subversive enemies. Even now we attempt to increase the vigilance of the so-called free world by pointing to the plight of the captive peoples of the Communist slave world.

If we keep in mind the idea that slavery is inherently destructive to liberty and is the inevitable punishment for communal apathy and disunity, we can clarify some of the curious ambiguities in the abolitionists' choice of language. Obviously Charles Sumner was thinking of more than the institution of Negro bondage when he said, in 1861, that the rebellion was not merely caused by slavery but "is Slavery itself, incarnate, living, acting, raging, robbing, murdering according to the essential law of its being." Seven years earlier he had charged that apologists for slavery were necessarily "abolitionists of freedom." William Goodell labored the same point with numerous citations from the Southern press, including reports of duels and lynching, harsh laws prescribing punishment for even published innuendos that might stir up the colored population, and official demands that Northern governors extradite abolitionist editors for trial and punishment under the laws of Southern states. "In no part of Europe, or even in Asia," Goodell claimed, "are the people subjected to a sterner despotism than are the *white* population of our own Southern States." After describing seven ways in which the Slave Power had eroded liberty in the North, Theodore Parker asserted that "slavery had privately emptied her seven vials of wrath upon the nation—committing seven debaucheries of human safeguards of our National Rights." The worst was yet to come: "This Apocalyptic Dragon, grown black with long-confined deeds of shame and death, now meditates five further steps of crime." Parker's numerology carried obvious overtones of Biblical prophecy, implying that through the process of history the Antichrist had at last been revealed. Parker explicitly affirmed that all Christendom was party to the contest; if slavery endured in America, democracy and every form of republic or constitutional monarchy would be sure to perish throughout the world. The unmistakable conclusion was that the Slave Power was a reincarnation of the same Jesuitical, anti-libertarian force which had directed the Counter-Reformation, subverted the British Constitution, corrupted the French Revolution, and blasted the hopes of every progressive movement in Europe. By mythologizing Negro slavery as a demonic power, abolitionists merged the objective institution with all the negative connotations of a loss of physical and spiritual freedom. Thus it was not simply a question of resisting the expansion of an undesirable labor system, but of preventing the enslavement—and indeed the Africanization—of the American people.[31]

So long as abolitionists retained faith in awakening slaveholders to the sinfulness of treating men as things, they could act on the assumptions and expectations of Protestant evangelists preaching to the unconverted. But even the most zealous missionaries had discovered the impossibility of converting appreciable numbers of Roman Catholics, or the adherents of any faith which had developed an exclusionist ideology and a self-protective discipline. According to Lyman Beecher, whose anti-Catholic crusade prefigured so many of the themes of his children's mission against slavery, it was not the personal character of individuals that had perverted the Catholic Church but rather "the system which perverted personal character." The Catholic system inevitably corrupted its leaders and debased and enslaved their followers. Similarly, abolitionists maintained that the Southern mind, nursed, educated, and daily exercised in tyranny, automatically lost the power of self-control. Carl Schurz, in a speech of 1860, asserted that while Southerners pretended to be free citizens, they were "by necessities arising from their condition, the slaves of slavery." [32]

These concepts of slavery and freedom were charged with religious overtones. The South "accepts Slavery," Theodore Parker said, "as the Dagon of its idolatry . . . and Slavery is to the South what the Book of Mormon or the car of Juggernaut is to its worshippers." Charles

Sumner complained in 1855 that the Founding Fathers could never have dreamed of "any oligarchical combination, constituting a mighty Propaganda, such as we now witness, to uphold and extend [slavery]." Like the mighty College of Propaganda of the Catholic Church (from which, incidentally, the term "propaganda" originates), the Slave Power systematically deluded its subjects, sealing off their minds from the cleansing currents of truth. George W. Curtis admitted that no thoughtful man would condemn indiscriminately all the inhabitants of the slave states or even all the owners of slaves; rather, attacks against slavery were directed toward a system. It was the system, Schurz maintained, which compelled Southerners to be disloyal to the Union. Since they had identified their social existence with the existence of slavery, they were compelled by the laws of self-preservation to suppress every disturbing or contradictory idea. "All [the Slave Power's] demands and acts are in strict harmony with its interests and attributes," he went on; "they are the natural growth of its existence." This argument of inevitability implied that slavery must either be accepted as an unalterable fact or destroyed root and branch. In neither case was there room for rational persuasion and gradual enlightenment.[33]

Moreover, it was not by intellectual subtlety but by duplicity and intimidation that the Slave Power supposedly controlled public opinion. A small oligarchy of Southern planters masked their true designs with rhetorical devotions to democracy and the Union. At the same time, they had concocted incidents like the nullification crisis of 1832–33 in order "to train the conscience and mind" of the Southern people. They had also bribed public officials, exploited ignorance and racial prejudice in both North and South, and organized violent mob demonstrations to silence criticism. "The politicians of the South" said William Henry Channing, "are a disciplined corps, schooled in the art of managing a small embodied force, so as to subjugate vast multitudes." John Gorham Palfrey explained how the wealthy Southern planters had acquired such power over their poorer neighbors: "When a small number of men in a community occupy a position such as to command respect and to make it easy for them to dispense useful services and acceptable attentions, it would be very strange if they did not get something of the character of oracles." Not only did the oracle have the economic power of employing overseers and mechanics, but he would give a bag of corn, a chicken, or a friendly word to the stranger who passed his gate. He was, in other words, the rural counterpart of the big city boss. In effect, Palfrey had turned the popular image of Southern gentility on its head.[34]

The planter class wielded power through its monopoly on knowledge as well as on property. It controlled the appointment and livelihood of teachers, postmasters, and village newspaper editors. It thrived on the ignorance and brutality of the poor whites. Slaveholders were proverbially arrogant and pugnacious, according to Josiah Quincy, because "such bullying is a sure path to popularity among their own constituents." In the spring of 1848, rioting mobs in Washington jeopardized the freedom of the press in the nation's capital. Palfrey blamed the Slave Power for directing the mobs' fury against the antislavery *National Era*. When Senator John P. Hale of New Hampshire asked leave to introduce a bill curbing riots and unlawful assemblies in the city, he received a blunt invitation from Senator Foote, which was soon referred to as an invitation to come to Mississippi and be hung. Only the President's willingness to keep the Marines on alert had saved the antislavery press from being suppressed by bullying tactics.[35] Even as far north as Utica, New York, the Slave Power had allegedly come close to annihilating civil liberties. This had been done by inflaming drunken ruffians with malicious propaganda and by spreading the doctrine that it was patriotic for the people to take the law into their own hands when legal safeguards protected the rights of fearless, and therefore unpopular social critics. In 1835 William Thomas voiced alarm over mob violence in Utica, which, he pointed out, coincided with national censorship of mail and outbreaks of lynching in the South. Postmaster General Amos Kendall, by approving the destruction of controversial mail, had given "the signal for general law-breaking." The tactics of lynch law were soon reduced to a deliberate system of terrorism, in which solid citizens would take the lead, pretending to uphold law and order, only to give free rein to hired thugs and drunken rabble who would carry mob violence to its predictable extremes.[36]

There can be no doubt that antislavery literature evoked an ugly backlash which seriously threatened the basic safeguards of a free society. By the mid-1830's thoughtful Americans had every reason to fear the tyrannical suppression of civil liberties. Yet the themes I have been discussing also touched a profound problem in American ideology. On the one hand, most Americans at least paid lip service to the Jeffersonian ideal that truth would be most secure where there were no restrictions on diversity, dissent, and even dangerous error. On the other hand, most educated men accepted the belief that character is shaped by environment and especially by political and social institutions. In the United States there were no transcendent national forces to check the conditioning influence of local environments. In the opinion of Carl Schurz, even the construction of the Constitution was determined by "the predominance of interests." As we have already seen, proslavery writers could endorse the principles of an open society while demanding the suppression of abolitionism as a subversive, un-American force which had been nourished by the selfish interests and decadent culture of the Northeast. Their antagonists could attack slavery as an institution, which, by corrupting its adherents and closing their minds to truth, inevitably undermined the foundations of a free society. Both sides practiced a form of ideological diagnosis that was a way of defining norms and thus of coming to terms with a basic problem of liberalism. In other words, the threat of diversity and environmental conditioning could be exorcised through projection to a negative reference group. Let me emphasize that the use of such psychological terms should not blind us to the objective contradictions of American slavery which were increasingly exposed through the process of controversy. But our focus here is on the meaning of the paranoid style as it sharply polarized men's perceptions. Konrad Lorenz has recently described patterns of group differentiation in both animals and men. From either biological or cultural conditioning, organisms frequently engage in a kind of ritualized ceremony which serves to suppress conflict within a given group, to hold it together as a unit, and to differentiate it, often through aggression, from other similar units.[37] It does not seem overly fanciful to see such a cultural ritualization in the slavery controversy, or to suggest that Americans increasingly used slavery as the primary symbol for defining the values and roles that would constitute their social identity. One may add that if a national fixation on this symbol involved extremes of aggression and guilt, the result was not without its poetic justice, given the historical connection between Negro slavery and the very foundations of American progress.

We have seen how both sides tried to associate their opponents with traditional enemies, such as foreign aristocrats or revolutionaries. Yet polarization soon made the domestic conspirator far more threatening than any foreign power. England, said Theodore Parker, is only our rival, even if sometimes a mean and dishonorable one (his grandfather had died at Lexington bridge); "But the South is our *foe*—far more dangerous, meaner, and more dishonorable. England keeps treaties; the South breaks faith. . . . Her success is our ruin." In another address in the 1850's Parker maintained that though the two sections shared a common history and ethnological origin, they had become "utterly diverse and antagonistic in disposition and aim. The North has organized Freedom, and seeks to extend it; the South, Bondage, and aims to spread that. The North is progressively Christian and democratic; while the South is progressively anti-Christian and undemocratic." [38]

Parker's stress on geographic differences tends to obscure a central cleavage in values, styles, and expectations that overlapped sectional boundaries. In 1854 Parker himself affirmed that "the idea which allows Slavery in South Carolina will establish it also in New England." The pivotal conflict was not between regions but between freedom and slavery, democracy and despotism. "You may cry 'Peace! Peace!,'" Parker said, "but so long as these two antagonistic Ideas remain, each seeking to . . . get exclusive power, there is no peace; there can be none." There was no "centre of gravity common to Freedom and Slavery." Abolitionists seldom forgot that the North had played an indispensable role in promoting the cause of the Slave Power. In 1836 a Rhode Island antislavery convention underscored the familiar point that it was now a struggle between the first principles of liberty and absolute despotism, and then observed that it was irrelevant "whether the Aristocracy of the North and the slaveholders of the South have literally combined together, for the overthrow of liberty, or whether they are drawn to act in concert by the operation of moral affinities or identity of interest. . . . It is sufficient to know the fact that they act together." [39]

Again we encounter the fear of being duped and manipulated by deceitful performances based on secret co-operation. Both parties to the slavery conflict exaggerated the backstage calculations of their opponents. Once men were disposed to perceive every event as part of a subtle and systematic plot, there was no room for accident, blunder, or human frailty. "The spirit of southern slavery," Garrison said, "is a spirit of EXTERMINATION against all those who dare represent it as a dishonor to our country, rebellion against God, and treason against the liberties of mankind." [40] When the stakes were so high, when the conflict absorbed and crystallized so many diffuse anxieties, one could make no charitable allowances. In an 1855 election speech at Faneuil Hall, Charles Sumner swept the deck clear of the petty political questions designed to distract men from the only important issue. "Are you for Freedom," he asked, "or are you for Slavery? . . . Are you for God, or are you for the Devil?" [41] And with these elemental terms, the paranoid style stripped off the last thin masks of ritualized drama and arrived at the ultimate symbols of polarization.

61

3

The Slave Power
and the Great American Enemy

Before analyzing the Slave Power thesis in greater depth,
it may be helpful to convey a clearer picture of the men
who were responsible for its elaboration and popularity.
I have already indicated that the image of a Slave Power
conspiracy became common currency, appropriated by
British journalists as well as by Southern opponents of
disunion. Yet it was a fairly small group of men—scarcely over twenty-five or thirty—who first delineated the
Slave Power in speeches, articles, and books, who drew on
one another's works, and who were more generally quoted as leading ideologues. A collective portrait of such
counter-subversives yields little support for explanatory
generalizations. One would be hard put to distinguish
this group from men of similar backgrounds who were
indifferent or friendly toward the slave system. But de-
scriptive generalization may help us avoid misconcep-
tions stemming from our own experience. It is my im-

pression, for example, that most twentieth-century practitioners of the paranoid style have been quite different types from the exposers of the Slave Power conspiracy.

Although our selected group contained a large proportion of men from high status and even nationally prominent families, such as the Adamses and Channings, there was an almost equal number with humble origins. Henry Wilson, to cite an extreme case, was the son of a day laborer and began his working life as an indentured servant. Despite such varied backgrounds, most of these antislavery men achieved exceptional levels of education, often at the nation's leading colleges. They benefited from either close family ties or the encouragement of older friends or professional mentors. While most had extensive religious nurture, often of a liberal variety, few were attracted to the ministry as a career. At least half received training in the law. A significant number evidenced a high degree of uncertainty over career, which was perhaps a mark of the changing professional patterns of their age, and of the role confusion which I discussed in my first lecture. While it is to be expected that such a sample would contain many professional writers, one is struck by the nearly universal experience of editing newspapers or journals. Whether he received training as a lawyer, doctor, or minister, our typical counter-subversive learned the ways of the world through journalism. He may have edited his own local paper or written for major national journals; in either case his style and perspective were those of the contemporary and increasingly cosmopolitan press, which had already adopted a pose of moralistic cynicism as it pursued its mission of unmasking frauds and of educating the gullible public. Unlike so many of the early abolitionists, he was strongly oriented toward politics. Our group embraces a wide variety of early political allegiances and political experimentation. But at least half of these enemies of the Slave Power were elected to state or national offices. And of course they came to constitute a central bloc in the Republican Party. They have often been accused, both in their own time and retrospectively, of cloaking political opportunism under a moralistic and hate-arousing crusade. But however we may judge their motives, they were clearly not misfits or marginal men. In terms of education, friendships, outgoing self-confidence, and social effectiveness, they were an intellectual elite of their generation.

Their attacks on the Slave Power were preoccupied with three broad themes which give important clues to some to the deeper fears and inner needs of Northern society. The first theme involved the meaning of American history and was essentially concerned with accounting for the gap between the patriotic images and ideals of schoolbook history and the guilt-laden heritage of Negro slavery. A second theme dealt with the moral ambiguities of American expansionism, and identified slavery as the central force endangering America's mission to save the world. The third theme emphasized the need for elevating and purifying society, for reviving a sense of communal solidarity in order to protect fundamental values from being subverted by slavery. I shall discuss each of these ideas in succession.

Antislavery writers had to come to terms with the knowledge that Negro bondage was hardly an innovation and that the institution had been at least tolerated by the Founding Fathers and by the Constitution itself. The indigenous character of the Slave Power raised serious problems, especially in a nation so convinced of its own millennial destiny under the special providence of God. In the 1790's it had been possible to style Jeffersonian Republicans as the dupes of a French plot to seize control of America. In the eyes of a New England Republican named Abraham Bishop, the hysteria over the Illuminati was itself the product of a conspiracy hatched by the British and by Alexander Hamilton, who was after all a foreigner.[1] But as we have seen, it was the defenders of slavery who could point to the English sources and English connections of the abolitionists.

One of the few attempts to portray the Slave Power as the mechanism of a foreign conspiracy was made, interestingly enough, by John C. Hamilton, who devoted most of his life to the vindication and idolization of his statesman father. In a speech written during the Civil War, he raked over his father's old grievances and paranoid suspicions, mixing the ashes of long-extinguished quarrels with the flaming hatred aroused by sectional conflict. Thus Hamilton asserted that it was no mere coincidence that foreign subversion first took root in Virginia, "the first great Slave State of the Union," that it was Virginia which originated disloyal opposition to Washington's Administration, and which propagated the heresy of secession. Despite John Hamilton's family-inspired obsessions, such as accusing Jefferson of conspiring with Citizen Genêt, his Manichaean version of American history elaborated many of the standard antislavery themes. Perhaps only a Hamilton gone sour could have labored the charge that Jefferson and Madison had been tools of the French as well as personifications of the Slave Power. But the thesis that Jeffersonian Republicans had deprived America of a strong national government and had tried to emasculate the Constitution by undercutting Hamilton's economic reforms laid a historical basis for the later view of the Slave Power conspiring to sabotage the Northern economy. Hamilton saw direct collusion between the Slave Power and various foreign enemies, especially in instigating the Whiskey Rebellion and in plotting secession and the Civil War. During the intervening decades, however, the Slave Power had apparently managed to manipulate commercial crises and political upheavals without benefit of foreign aid.[2]

If the Slave Power was to be conceptualized as a diabolical force similar to Illuminism, Masonry, and Catholicism, how was one to explain its emergence from native roots? One might claim that the conspiracy was of recent origin and that the South had suddenly fallen into the hands of a small faction of unscrupulous men, who would thus be analogous, in the imagery of countersubversion, to the scheming bankers of the 1830's, to the later Wall Street manipulators, or to New Dealers and the modern "liberal establishment." For a time many antislavery writers tried to pinpoint some dramatic turning point, such as Polk's nomination or the annexation of Texas, which signaled a great betrayal and an abrupt confrontation between freedom and bondage. Yet Negro slavery implicated the entire South; its history went back to the first colonial settlements. Much as the Vietnam War has led modern radicals into a reexamination of America's earlier and supposedly altruistic involvement in world affairs, so the crisis over slavery in the territories forced abolitionist writers to reconsider the entire sweep of American history in the light of Slave Power subversion.

The Reverend Frederick Frothingham discovered that two deadly foes, the ideas of liberty and of slavery, had been planted at the same time in the new continent's virgin soil. "Slavery," said Henry Wilson, "from the day it entered the harbor of Jamestown . . . was an alien in America, an enemy to law and order, liberty and progress." Always seductive as well as aggressive, it had "glided into the illustrious assembly that proclaimed America independent." Theodore Parker projected the Manichaean vision on an even wider screen. America had been "the last new continent left as a stage for the development of mankind." In this cosmic drama, one troupe of actors consisted of Anglo-Saxon Puritans who carried on the spirit of progressive emancipation inaugurated by the Protestant Reformation. The Spanish, as the opposing players, not only brought to the stage "the superstition and tyranny of mediaeval Europe," but re-invented "the old sin" of Negro slavery, which was soon implanted in Virginia. Parker conceded that Latin America did not extend to the Potomac, but slavery was the rhetorical emblem which identified Southerners with Spanish despotism. Although European despotism had been "the angel which strengthened the colonies during the Revolution," the union was "only military—for defence." Once the external threat was removed, commercial expediency was the only remaining basis for union.[3]

The Founding Fathers, it appeared, had been a bit naive about potential sources of corruption (Washington, after all, had been duped by the Freemasons as well as by the Slave Power). As John Gorham Palfrey pointed out, the authors of the Constitution had recognized the vulnerability of former republics and had taken every precaution to protect America's freedom from a future nobility or established church. Unfortunately, they had been blind to the most dangerous and native source of aristocratic power. What Joshua Leavitt termed the "ill-advised concessions" of the Constitutional Convention had laid the groundwork for "a long series of usurpations on the one hand and surrenders on the other." It was at the Constitutional Convention, said the Frenchman Augustin Cochin, that "the monstrous nuptials of liberty and servitude were hallowed." By allowing "the fatal flaw" of slavery to continue, the Fathers had "provided the seed of destruction in the very birth of the Union." [4]

As William Goodell and other abolitionists looked back on American history from the vantage point of the 1840's, everything fell into a meaningful pattern. What had seemed haphazard confusion, or in Goodell's words, "the inexplicable labyrinths of American politics for the last sixty years," suddenly clarified as a systematic plot. The nation's founders had overlooked the great moral truth "that the tolerance of sin leads to corruption, and that usurpation ever grows by submission and is never satisfied." Although the South soon fell far behind the North in both wealth and civilization, "the Slave Power, like the power of the pit, never lacks for a stratagem." By holding the balance of power between political parties, the slave oligarchy, according to William Henry Channing, had successfully intrigued "to elect Presidents and Vicepresidents, Speakers of the House of Representatives, Secretaries of State, Treasury, and War, Chiefs of Army and Navy, Judges of the Supreme Court and foreign Ambassadors." They had forced through Congress disgraceful legislation discriminating against free American blacks. They had taken President Jefferson by the hand, in the words of James C. Jackson, "and under a pretext of securing a free navigation of the Mississippi, made him violate his principles of constitutional construction," in order to acquire the vast domain of Louisiana for slavery's expansion. It was no accident that an embargo and needless war had crippled Northeastern commerce soon after the slave trade had been abolished and a New Englander had exposed Aaron Burr's great Southwestern conspiracy (which, we might add, had earlier been blamed on the Freemasons). Nor was it fortuitous that Southern officers in the War of 1812 had prevented the brave soldiers of New England and New York from capturing Canada. "Had Canada been adjacent to the Slave States," Goodell wrote, ". . . there can be no reasonable doubt that it could have been conquered as expeditiously as were California and New Mexico." [5]

Apparently meaningless fluctuations in national policy had been engineered to disrupt and break down the Northern economy. The Slave Power had established the Second Bank in order to drain capital from the North; after pillaging the bank, the Slave Power had destroyed it. The two-party system had been cunningly contrived to divert attention from important issues and to conceal the backstage machinations of America's true rulers. Thus the electorate had been divided by specious controversies, never realizing, for example, that the depression of 1837 had been caused by slaveholder indebtedness and by the steady drain of Northern surplus wealth into the Southwest. Goodell claimed that Calhoun himself had furnished the key for unlocking the secrets of recent political history. "The free North," Calhoun was quoted as saying, "must be shorn of her own natural strength, when needful, that slavery may preserve her balance of power." [6]

During the long period when Calhoun had presided, in Channing's phrase, as "the Grand-Master of the conspirators," the Slave Power had met resistance from only a small band of despised abolitionists. In 1855 Charles

70

Francis Adams confessed that he had once had little sympathy for "the heroic few, who saw more clearly into the depth of the evil, [and] understood that time, instead of approximating the freedom of the slave, threatened to fasten fetters upon themselves." From the perspective of the 1850's, it was difficult to keep from mythologizing the early heroes who had struggled against "the press, the politicians, the merchants, the lawyers, the church, the government, and its army of dependents of every sort, and, lastly . . . the popular prejudices against the slaves because they were black." To blame abolitionists for causing the Civil War, said Charles Sumner, was like blaming Christian martyrs for the tortures imposed by heathens. In a society of hypocrites, they had been the models of sincerity and authentic action.[7]

Antislavery historians agreed that the Slave Power had directed national policy and had achieved its successive goals until Kansas voters overwhelmingly rejected the Lecompton Constitution. Some writers charged that a small group of secessionists had originally seized upon the repeal of the Missouri Compromise as "an entering wedge which would sooner or later enable them to split the Union." Others felt that the Slave Power, drugged by a long career of success, had been unprepared for the setback in Kansas. In any event, the Kansas defeat had immediately put in motion a network of conspiracies in the government and armed services preparing for a *coup d'état* and overthrow of the Republic. As chairman of the Senate Committee on Military Affairs, Jefferson Davis conspired with the Secretary of the Army, John B. Floyd, plundering the Treasury and transferring huge quantities of arms and munitions from the Northern states to the South. "Never before in any country," Sumner wrote, "was there a similar crime, which embraced so many persons in the highest places of power or which took within its grasp so large a theatre of human action." [8]

A rigorous analysis of this antislavery historiography would doubtless reveal hard grains of truth connected with a mucilage of exaggeration and fantasy. But the central theme, which is so central to the paranoid style, is the conviction that an exclusive monolithic structure has imposed a purposeful pattern on otherwise unpredictable events. One suspects that this conviction is a product of the liberal faith, inherited from the Enlightenment, that history *can* be shaped in accordance with a rational plan. When such a comforting expectation is continually shattered by wars, depressions, and social injustice, it is natural to assume that some evil force is at work. When the irrationality of events proves that the children of light have lost control, then the children of darkness must have secretly seized the levers of history. The illusion of American omnipotence, as Denis Brogan once suggested, easily leads to a fear of un-American omnipotence.

This brings me to my second theme, which concerns the relation between Slave Power expansionism and America's mission to save the world. The Slave Power's most frightening trait, according to numerous writers, was an insatiable lust which successive victories only further inflamed. "The Slave Power," wrote Carl Schurz, "is impelled by the irresistible power of necessity. It cannot exist unless it rules, and it cannot rule unless it keeps down its opponents." Like European despotism and the Catholic Inquisition, Schurz added, "slavery demands extension by an aggressive foreign policy." [9] Inevitable expansionism suggested the metaphor of the entering wedge, which had been worn smooth in the rhetoric of earlier counter-subversion. Thus, William Seward had told an 1830 convention of anti-Masons: "We will not wait for the accomplishment of this scheme of tyranny. Did our forefathers wait? Three cents tax upon a pound of *tea* was a small matter; but it was the entering wedge, which this community would not suffer to be applied to the fabric of her liberties." In 1851 Palfrey employed the same figure to describe Louisiana's admission to statehood: "The wedge was well entered, and in due time came the sturdy blows of the beetle to drive it further in." The blows would not stop, moreover, until slavery had won legal protection in all the states and until a great empire of slavery, to paraphrase William Henry Channing, stretched from the Atlantic to the Pacific, and from the snows of Canada to the Caribbean or even the Amazon.[10]

Metaphor dramatized the picture of slavery as a power that could never be limited by compromise. As early as 1830 the *New England Weekly Review* stated that "all are aware that the slavery which exists in these states is a deadly and cancerous sore upon the vitals of the commonwealth—that it must be eradicated—or the nation dies!" The virgin lands of the West, whose vast resources offered such hope to mankind, were imperiled by the leprous disease of slavery. "We cannot escape its presence," said George Julian, "without forsaking the country. We inhale it at every breath, and imbibe it at every pore. We 'live, and move and have our being' in the midst of this frightful moral pestilence, which is hovering like a dark cloud over the land, and menacing the very life of the Republic." Slavery was a giant parasite, a plague, a poisonous plant, a dragon, a monster. Unless met and totally exterminated, warned Nathaniel P. Bailey, it would "soon prove the Angel of Death to this first-born of Christian Republics." In 1861, six years after this utterance, Charles Sumner likened the rebellion of the fallen slavemasters of the Republic to that "earliest Rebellion by the fallen spirits against the Almighty Throne." [11]

Such religious allusions were a good deal more than rhetorical flourishes. The symbols men use often shape their perception of events. For American Protestants who had lost faith in the revealed word of God, the slavery conflict was itself a revelation which reanimated religious symbols and provided a new sense of historical identity and purpose. Consider the implications of the following imagery, taken from a speech by Charles D. Drake: "The conflict is . . . as irrepressible as that between good and evil, . . . between truth and falsehood, between Heaven and Hell." The South "made of slavery 'AN IMAGE OF GOLD,' and 'set it up in the plain' . . . and because the

74

North would not 'fall down and worship the golden image,' that this Southern 'Nebuchadnezzar had set up,' decreed that this noble country should 'be cast into the midst of the burning fiery furnace' of this cruel and devouring war. This, my friends, is God's own truth." The freedom to assail slavery, Drake maintained, was "now as irrefragable a right, as the freedom to worship God according to the dictates of conscience." In other words, the discovery of America's great enemy revealed a national mission that was at one with the epic struggles of the past. It was a struggle, said Frederick Frothingham, not only "of Order with Disorder, of Self-sacrifice with Selfishness, of Civilization with Barbarism . . . [but] of God with Satan." Slavery was a black Goliath defying the Lord. "If David fall," Frothingham predicted, "the progress of mankind is turned backward, the lessons of history are unlearned, and the human race for centuries to come must wander in darkness, and wade through seas of blood to regain the point where it now stands." [12]

Theodore Parker reminded his listeners in Boston that it had been three hundred years since their fathers in Europe had contended for freedom of conscience; two hundred years had elapsed since the overthrow of monarchic despotism in England; nearly a century had passed since the American colonists had begun defending the rights of man. Each of these great steps toward mankind's salvation was now in jeopardy. We have not sufficiently appreciated that for many American Protestants, the Reformation, even more than the Revolution, was the model of a timeless, archetypal experience that had to be reenacted, in almost ritualistic fashion, if freedom was to be preserved. Freedom, in each of Parker's examples, implied a deliverance, a ripping off of veils and cloaks, an abolition of secrecy and monopolistic powers, an opening of the soul to the withheld word of God. "The Church," said George Julian, "I fully believe, is to redeem the race. But as in ancient days, so now, the work of reform must begin outside of existing systems . . . among the great body of the people. We must not begin with the chief priests and rulers, who are always ready to crucify Reform, but like Fox and Wesley take our stand in the midst of the multitude, who have no other interest than to find and embrace the truth." Repeatedly the opponents of the Slave Power likened their stand to that of Protestant reformers from Luther to Wesley, and thought of their crusade as a reenactment of sacred struggles against the Kingdom of Darkness.[13]

The institution of Negro slavery perfectly conformed to the inherited image of the Antichrist. It awakened millenarian fantasies of persecution and suffering, of absolute power and absolute emancipation from the very principle of violence. The government's sanction of a slaveholder's dominion seemed analogous to a government's sanction of a priest's authority over his parishioner. Like the priest, the slaveholder withheld the Bible and nullified the marriage covenant. According to Parker, "as the Catholic priest takes a bit of baker's bread, and says, 'Bread, thou art, become a God!' and the dough is

God,—so the South takes any man and transubstantiates him,—'Thou art a man! become a President!' And by political transubstantiation Polk and Pierce are Presidents, to be 'lifted up,' and to be 'exhibited,' set on high, and worshipped accordingly." When Northern ministers were told that slavery was a political question which was beyond the province of the church, they could reply that the so-called politics of the French Revolution, which had been controlled by ex-Jesuit Illuminati, had led to an official denial of God and of immortality, to legalized brothels and licentiousness.[14]

There has often been an element of projection in the idea of an enemy's expansionism. Thus the fear of an international Catholic conspiracy justified the most strenuous and dedicated efforts at the evangelical conquest of the West. Lyman Beecher's picture of Catholic expansionism, in his influential book *A Plea for the West*, was in reality a mirror image of his own aspirations for New England Protestant culture. Beecher even admitted that much unintended good would come out of Popery, which had at last awakened the Protestant missionary spirit. The threat of a competing enemy was certain proof of New England's mission to expand westward and ultimately to save the world. Attacks on the Slave Power were frequently mixed with similarly grandiose visions of America's destiny. The expansion of slavery was to be met not by containment but by the expansion of freedom, which meant the institutions and moral values of Northeastern Protestant society. In effect, polarization allowed Nor-

77

therners to project on the Slave Power all the guilt and negative connotations of imperial expansion. It was the Slave Power that was responsible for the Louisiana Purchase, the Seminole War, Indian removal, and the bullying of Mexico. Yet antislavery writers had no doubts about America's being "the heir of all the ages," with a God-given responsibility toward mankind. The annihilation of slavery, indeed, was to be the essential preparatory step toward the extension of an empire of liberty and benevolence around the globe.[15]

But the American way of life was hardly worth extending unless the people succeeded, as William Seward put it, in restoring "the demoralized virtue of the nation." Our third theme, the urgent need for internal purification, was dramatically defined by a Rhode Island antislavery convention of 1836. In an address to professing Christians who were praying for India and other benighted countries, the abolitionists asked, "will you pray and labor for the conversion, the social, intellectual, and religious elevation of all the nations of the earth, excepting our own?" Such a course would inevitably bring a retributive judgement from the Lord.[16]

Northern alarmists insisted that the Slave Power's triumphs in external expansion had been matched, and largely caused by, the internal disintegration of free society. In very similar fashion the external successes of communism after World War II were associated with the moral decay of American society, which meant, at least for certain extremists, that communists had promoted modern

78

art and uncensored sex to confuse and divide the common people. The Slave Power, though also bent on demoralizing the national character, had not needed to rely on dangerous ideas and revolutionary cultural forms. It was sufficient to exploit the North's great flaw of subordinating life to material gain. "The clink of the dollar," said Parker, "—that is the *reveille*, the morning drum-beat, for the American people." Whereas slaveholders were united, according to Parker, and were at least true to their own institution and their own ideal, most Northerners, in their selfish pursuit of wealth, had lost any sense of communal purpose.[17]

The call for internal purification was a way of rejecting the prevailing political consensus, particularly its capacity for expedient compromise and its lack of moral commitment. In addition, the identification of specific targets of subversion was a means of reaffirming popular faith in the central institutions of Protestant democracy. Thus, public schools, the local church, free speech, a free press, and the family homestead acquired heightened value when seen as the key targets of Catholic or Slave Power conspiracies.

But in a more general sense, appeals for communal regeneration retraced patterns that had descended from Puritan jeremiad sermons to the evangelical revivals. As Perry Miller has observed, religious revivals depended on a presumed declension of faith, on the corruption and backsliding of each younger generation. The miracle of social awakening required a resistant force of infidelity.

79

We should not be surprised, therefore, to find anti-Masonry praised as a regenerative force, comparable to the Reformation and the American Revolution, whose mission lay in counteracting apathy and self-seeking. Samuel F. B. Morse frankly preached anti-Catholicism as a means of ending Protestant disunity and restoring the cohesive spirit of the Founding Fathers. William Henry Channing predicted that the intolerable exactions of the Slave Power would be the means for renovating the national conscience. Perhaps the arrogant slave masters were right in assuming that the Northern masses were cowardly, disheartened, and disunited, and that the merchants and bankers had been corrupted by worldliness and love of gain. But the Slave Power had underestimated the power of the revivalist tradition. In the words of Rhode Island abolitionists, "the sons of Roger Williams will take and communicate the alarm, and a nation of freemen, we trust, will be aroused to their danger." [18]

It was not fortuitous that Paul Revere and the Minutemen became the evocative symbols of the American Revolution. Through the entire literature of counter-subversion one encounters repeated references to the stupidity and docility of the people of Europe, who in the last analysis deserved their enslavement to church and state. European tyrants seemed able to crush every democratic conspiracy, so that force alone determined the destiny of peoples. In America, therefore, it was necessary to institutionalize the first revolutionary conspiracy *of* the people, as a ready weapon against potential tyrants.

It was a fatal mistake to rely on the mere forms of republican government, trusting in laws and in the reputation of leaders. Cassius Clay exposed the hollowness of American pretenses to freedom: "The Pope says: discuss freely all subjects, but don't touch with profane hands, holy things—don't canvass religion! There is no liberty, then, in Popedom. . . . The United States say: abuse, if you please, the Pope; denounce the Czar; don't spare the iniquities of British aristocracy and oppression; but don't interfere with *slavery*—that's a *delicate relation* . . . let that alone, or we'll Lynch you! There is, then, no *liberty in America*. So long as there is one thing in a nation which cannot be discussed—there is no freedom of speech or the press in that nation." [19]

Only by such denunciations of communal backsliding could America's special destiny be fulfilled. The jeremiad sermon, religious or secular, was the only means of restoring the purity of original principles, and thus of combatting the moral erosion of history. In the eyes of Joshua Leavitt, the Union had become a conquered province of the South, "and all this is so because the people choose to have it so. It is because slavery has blinded the eyes of the people, as well as corrupted the hearts of politicians of all parties." Whereas America had been born to a special mission, it had now become as abjectly submissive to "this invincible usurped power" as Canada was to Great Britain. If fire-and-brimstone preachers held out only a few precious moments when salvation might be won, their abolitionist counterparts warned that there was scarcely more time for the people to rouse themselves and resist the monster which, as Beriah Green said, had been fattened with Negro blood and "now opens his jaws and clamors for white victims." [20]

As these samples suggest, the abolitionist jeremiad was an instrument for castigating the existing political and economic structure for its dependence on expediency and self-interest. The purification sermon was also a way of bringing a higher scale of values to bear on a system ruled by consensus and compromise. The image of a slave oligarchy monopolizing Southern wealth and power led men like Palfrey and Julian to the discovery that the North itself was controlled by a cohesive mercantile and manufacturing interest. The reason why the Slave Power had easily won a dominant influence in the North was that the entire institutional structure was geared to the pursuit of wealth and office. There were not five colleges in all the North, Parker complained, that would publicly take a stand for freedom. The Northern churches were "slavery's city of refuge," her pulpits were slavery's "watch-towers." To the poor of the world, America's clergy preached not a gospel of hope but of captivity. The great tract, missionary, and Bible societies voluntarily accepted the yoke of Slave Power censorship. The Eastern money power, hungering for subsidies and favorable tariffs, courted the political power of the South. Heretics and nonconformists were quickly disciplined by economic pressure from the financiers; and since wealth set the fashion in Northern society, the aspiring classes and *nouveaux riches* flaunted their acceptance of slavery as a badge of status.[21]

In Julian's words, "no mere politicians can face the slaveholders and live. The slightest resistance to their sovereign will is enough to expel him forthwith from the paradise of office and power." Given the grandiose visions of America's millennial destiny, the ironic reference to politicians in paradise carried a bitter sting. In reality, the two major parties were "the surviving effects of causes now no longer operative, and have therefore no apology for their existence." A Democrat, said Parker, "is but a Whig on time; a Whig is a Democrat arrived at maturity." The old issues of banking, tariffs, and land distribution were now dismissed as profoundly irrelevant.[22]

Many antislavery writers seemed more concerned with the amorality of political parties and the sluggishness of public opinion than with the actual threat of the Slave Power. Even worse than the sin of slaveholding, Julian charged, were the actions of Northern politicians to uphold a monstrous system of oppression, "levying war against the institutions of their fathers." The proof of the political system's bankruptcy was its inability to resist the Slave Power. "Here," Julian said, "is the unclean spirit that must be cast out from the hearts of the people before they can be saved. We must enter the inner sanctuary of their consciences, and dispel the gathering clouds of passion and prejudice which hold them in the slumber of unconscious guilt. We must sound it incessantly in their ears, and in trumpet tones, that by remaining in the service of these [party] factions they are guilty of the untold wrongs of slavery." [23]

In this apocalyptic utterance we have the key for understanding the peculiarly religious character of many of the movements of counter-subversion, which is to say the desire to save apparently blameless men by raising their guilt to the level of consciousness. The image of the Slave Power was a vehicle for bringing to the surface some of the internal strains and conflicts of a liberal society. Only by arousing people to the menace of an absolute despotism could the inner sanctuary of individuality be breached and a cohesive community created.

We have analyzed the themes of corrupted and inaccessible minds, of an expansionist force whose entering wedges lead to unconditional enslavement, and of a radical need for purification and rededication. Since all three ideas run through the literature of anti-Masonry, anti-Mormonism, anti-Catholicism, and antislavery, we may suspect that they tell as much about the internal problems of a free society as about external conflicts of status and interest. Whatever the actual practices of slaveholders, priests, Masons, and Illuminati, the image of a tyrannical, conspiratorial force has helped liberals to define and work out the implications of their own values. Social purpose and identity, in other words, have been shaped by identifying the perfect enemy. And for a liberal, Protestant culture, slavery, whether physical, religious, or ideological, has been the root concept of opposition.

84

We might conclude, then, that the image of the Slave Power was a necessary means for arousing the fears and galvanizing the will of the North to face a genuine moral and political challenge. There is something almost providential in the way that the paranoid style, for all its irrationality, finally enabled significant numbers of Americans to perceive the evil of an institution which had long been intertwined with the promise of American life. I say "providential" because of the apparent coincidence of internal needs and external responsibility.

But the Slave Power image was also associated with certain dangerous assumptions which have by no means disappeared from American thought and which may be thought of as the natural outgrowth of the themes we have already examined. These assumptions are epitomized, I would suggest, in Mark Twain's *Connecticut Yankee in King Arthur's Court*, a novel that has more to do with nineteenth-century slavery than has commonly been supposed. First, our champions of freedom have shared the Yankee's easy confidence that if he were once transported to the center of despotism, he could open the souls and minds of the people to regenerative truth. Except for a few wicked Merlins or Morgan le Fe's, the people, as Julian had emphasized, had "no other interest than to find and embrace the truth." The American liberal ethic was so self-evident and sensible that it would dissolve the hold of church or slave owner, break Circe's spell of dehumanization, and presumably convert debased slaves into free and self-respecting beings. It was inconceivable to Twain's Yankee that anyone should resist being civilized.

A second assumption, which the Yankee's failures only gradually revealed, was that there could be no peaceful coexistence with the Antichrist. For if the Yankee could not realize his grandiose vision of saving history from the force of slavery, if he found all England marching against him and his fifty-two liberated youths, he was prepared to take the most desperate step: "I touched a button," he said, "and shook the bones of England loose from her spine. In that explosion all our noble civilization-factories went up in the air and disappeared from the earth. It was a pity, but it was necessary." The only alternative to the Yankee's civilization was annihilation.

Notes

Notes to Chapter 1

[1] Richard Hofstadter, *The Paranoid Style in American Politics and Other Essays* (New York, 1965), 3–40.

[2] For a fuller discussion of distinctive American styles or patterns, see my articles, "Some Themes of Counter-Subversion: An Analysis of Anti-Masonic, Anti-Catholic, and Anti-Mormon Literature," *Mississippi Valley Historical Review*, XLVII (September, 1960), 205–24, and "Some Ideological Functions of Prejudice in Ante-Bellum America," *American Quarterly*, XV (Summer, 1963), 115–25.

[3] Bernard Bailyn, *The Ideological Origins of the American Revolution* (Cambridge, Mass., 1967), 144–59. During the Civil War, Orville J. Victor sought to cash in on a timely topic and published a fat volume entitled, *History of American Conspiracies ... from 1760 to 1860* (New York, 1863), consisting of unrelated sketches of Pontiac's Conspiracy, Benedict Arnold, Shays's Rebellion, Nat Turner, and so on. Victor offered no theory of conspiracy and succeeded in showing only that internal violence had been common throughout American history.

[4] *History of the Plots and Crimes of the Great Conspiracy to Overthrow Liberty in America* (New York, 1866).

[5] One must remember that suspicion of poisoning (and perhaps the use of poison by murderers) was more common when medical diagnosis was in an extremely crude state. All guests left

87

the National Hotel after the initial epidemic and then returned in mid-February, when warmer weather seemed to alleviate the disease. In late February the illness returned with cold weather, leaving hundreds sick during the pre-inauguration ceremonies. The rumors of poisoning at the National Hotel were attributed to a malevolent waiter. See New York *Times*, March 10, 18, 23, 25, April 3, May 4, 9, 11, 15, July 3, 15; New York *Herald*, February 25, 26, March 2; Washington *Evening Star*, February 3, 27, March 20, 21, 25, April 2, 7; *National Era*, March 26.

[6] Robert Welch, *The New Americanism and Other Speeches and Essays* (Boston, 1966), 117–40.

[7] Dyer Burgess, *Anti-Conspirator, or, Infidelity Unmasked* (Cincinnati, 1832).

[8] James Otis, *The Rights of the British Colonists Asserted and Proved* (Boston, 1764), 34–35, 44–46, 57.

[9] Thomas Branagan, *Serious Remonstrances, Addressed to the Citizens of the Northern States* (Philadelphia, 1805), xiii, 57. While admitting that power had not corrupted every slaveholder, any more than every monarch, David Barrow affirmed that most monarchs and slaveholders were cruel and bad. See *Involuntary, Unmerited, Perpetual, Absolute, Hereditary Slavery, Examined* (Lexington, Ky., 1808), 22–26. In a valuable article which appeared soon after these lectures were written, Larry Gara dissociates abolitionism, based on a "humanitarian consideration for the slave as an oppressed human being," from the later political opposition to the Slave Power. This distinction helps explain how racism could be combined with a variety of antislavery. But one must emphasize that there were elements of the Slave Power thesis in early abolitionism, and that later opponents of the Slave Power could express a humanitarian concern for the slave. See Larry Gara, "Slavery and the Slave Power: A Crucial Distinction," *Civil War History*, XV (March, 1969), 5–18.

[10] Robert Ernst, *Rufus King, American Federalist* (Chapel Hill, 1968), 369–75; Ernst, "Rufus King, Slavery, and the Missouri Crisis," *New York Historical Society Quarterly*, XLVI (October, 1962), 357–82; Glover Moore, *The Missouri Controversy, 1819–1821* (Lexington, Ky., 1953), 79.

[11] *Genius of Universal Emancipation*, No. 1 (July, 1821).

[12] Merton C. Dillon, *Benjamin Lundy and the Struggle for Negro Freedom* (Urbana, Ill., 1966).

[13] See, for example, New Orleans City Council, *Report of a Conspiracy to Incite Rebellion Throughout the Slave States* (n.p., n.d.). The captured conspirator was John A. Murrell.

[14] William Goodell (ed.), *Anti-Slavery Lecturer,* I (Utica, N.Y., September, 1839).

[15] *Blackwood's Edinburgh Magazine,* LXXXIII (London, January, 1853), 17; John Elliot Cairnes, *The Slave Power: Its Character, Career and Probable Designs* (New York, 1862), 25–26.

[16] Charles Francis Adams, *What Makes Slavery a Question of National Concern? A Lecture, Delivered, by Invitation, at New York, January 30, and at Syracuse, February 1, 1855* (n.p., n.d.), 27.

[17] [George W. Allen], *The Complaint of Mexico, and Conspiracy Against Liberty* (Boston, 1843), 26.

[18] George W. Julian, "The Strength and Weakness of the Slave Power—the Duty of Anti-Slavery Men," in *Speeches on Political Questions* (New York, 1872), 70.

[19] George M. Weston, *Will the South Dissolve the Union?* (n.p., 1856), 3, 6.

[20] Charles D. Drake, *The Proclamation of Emancipation: Speech of Charles D. Drake, Delivered in Turners' Hall, St. Louis, January 28, 1863* (n.p., n.d.), 1.

[21] John Minor Botts, *The Great Rebellion: Its Secret History, Rise, Progress, and Disastrous Failure* (New York, 1866), *passim.* Botts was imprisoned by the Confederacy, and in 1866 organized a Union Republican Party in Virginia. See also, *Address of the Democratic State Central Committee together with the Proceedings of the Democratic State Convention Held at Harrisburg, July 4, 1862* (Philadelphia, 1862), 5.

[22] James W. Hunnicutt, *The Conspiracy Unveiled, the South Sacrificed; or, the Horrors of Secession* (Philadelphia, 1863), *passim.*

[23] *The Washington Despotism Dissected in Articles from the "Metropolitan Record"* (New York, 1863), 71–72, 106. Also, James A. Bayard, *Executive Usurpation: Speech of Hon. James A. Bayard of Delaware—July 19, 1861* (Washington, n.d.), 21. One should note that the war elicited a host of books and pamphlets exposing seditious and conspiratorial organizations in both the Union and Confederacy. Northern writers were particularly alarmed by various guerrilla or fifth-column groups such as the

Notes to Chapter 1

Knights of the Golden Circle and the Order of the Sons of Liberty. See Felix G. Stidger, *Treason: History of the Order of Sons of Liberty* (n.p., 1903); Benn Pitman, *The Trials for Treason at Indianapolis, Disclosing the Plans for Establishing a North-Western Confederacy* (Cincinnati, 1865); Hunnicutt, *Conspiracy Unveiled*, 247 ff.

24 Robert W. Doherty, "Status Anxiety and American Reform: Some Alternatives," *American Quarterly*, XIX (Summer, 1967), 329–37.

25 *The Presentation of Self in Everyday Life* (Garden City, N.Y., 1959), 35.

26 *Ibid.*, 105.

27 *Ibid.*, 164.

28 *Ibid.*, 132.

29 Lucy Smith, *History of the Prophet Joseph* (Salt Lake City, 1902), 74.

Notes to Chapter 2

1 Northern newspaper editors, particularly James Gordon Bennett and James Watson Webb, played an important role in portraying the abolitionists as subversives and as tools of the British.

2 [William Drayton], *The South Vindicated from the Treason and Fanaticism of Northern Abolitionists* (Philadelphia, 1836), 158.

3 James Hamilton, *An Account of the Late Intended Insurrection Among a Portion of the Blacks of this City* (Charleston, 1822), 6, 29–30.

4 New Orleans City Council, *Report of a Conspiracy to Incite Rebellion Throughout the Slave States* (n.p., n.d.), 1.

5 Edmund Ruffin, "Consequences of Abolition Agitation," *DeBow's Review*, XXII (1857), 588.

6 Albert Bledsoe, *Essay on Liberty and Slavery* (Philadelphia, 1856), 125; Duff Green, *Facts and Suggestions* (New York, 1866), 32, 45; Thomas Hart Benton, *Thirty Years View* (New York, 1856), 576.

7 John C. Calhoun, *Speeches* (New York, 1843), 215, 220.

8 [Drayton], *South Vindicated*, xv–xvii, 71; Joseph C. Stiles, *The National Controversy; or the Voice of the Fathers Upon the State of the Country* (New York, 1861), 53, 56.

9 Benton, *Thirty Years View*, 282–84.

10 Reprinted in William Goodell (ed.), *Anti-Slavery Lecturer* (September, 1839).

11 *Speech of Mr. Clement Claiborne Clay, Jr., of Alabama on the Contest in Kansas and the Plan and Purpose of Black Republicanism, 21 April, 1856* (Washington, n.d.), 12.

12 B. F. Stringfellow, *Negro-Slavery No Evil; or the North and the South* (St. Louis, 1854), 5–6; *National Era*, December 14, 1854; *Speech of the Hon. A. G. Brown, of Missouri, on the President's Kansas Message* (Washington, 1858), 9; [John Townsend], *The Doom of Slavery in the Union: Its Safety Out of It* (Charleston, S.C., 1860), 4–5, 10, 16, 34, 36–37.

13 [M. L. Hurlbut], "Anti-Abolitionists," *Christian Examiner*, XXIV (1838), 400; Calvin Colton, *Abolition a Sedition* (Philadelphia, 1839), 5, 13, 35, 60.

14 "Letter of Governor Shannon to President Pierce," in *The Kansas Question* (Washington, 1856), 16; *Conspiracy Disclosed!! Kansas Affairs. Read! Read!! Read!!!* (Washington, n.d.), 1–3, 5, 10.

15 *Speech of Mr. William Russell Smith of Alabama, on the Kansas Contested Election* (Washington, 1856), 3.

16 "The Periodical Press of the United States," *Southern Quarterly Review*, I (1842), 54; *Speech of William Russell Smith*, 4; *Speech of Clement Claiborne Clay, Jr.*, 18.

17 *Correspondence of Robert Toombs, Alexander Stephens, and Howell Cobb, Annual Report of the American Historical Association*, II (Washington, 1913), 351–53; *Speech of Robert Toombs of Georgia, on the President's Kansas Message* (Washington, 1856), 11.

18 *Correspondence of Robert Toombs, et al.*, 351–53; Stringfellow, *Negro Slavery No Evil*, 31; "Python" [pseud.], "The Relative Political Status of the North and South," *DeBow's Review*, XXII (1857), 117, 120. The fact that some abolitionists like Henry S. Wilson moved from the Know-Nothing Party to the Republican Party gave added credence to Southern charges. It should be noted that some critics saw the French Jacobins as prototypes of

the Know-Nothings. See, for example, *A Few Words to the Thinking and Judicious Voters of Pennsylvania* (n.p., 1854), 28.

[19] *Speech of Mr. Jabez L. M. Curry, of Alabama—Admission of Kansas, February 23, 1858* (Washington, n.d.), 5, 8; "Abolition and Sectarian Mobs," *United States Review*, XXXIV (August, 1854), 97, 103, 107–10; "Periodical Press of the United States," 54.

[20] "How the Wounded Pigeons Flutter," from the *National Advocate*, July 23, 1862 (New Orleans), 26; [Drayton], *South Vindicated*, 154; Green, *Facts and Suggestions*, 27, 32, 34, 36, 40, 48; [Charles G. Greene and B. F. Hallett], "The Identity of the Old Hartford Convention Federalists with the Modern Whig, Harrison Party," Boston *Morning Post, Extra* . . . , August, 1840, pp. 9, 13, 16; S. M. Johnson, *The Dual Revolutions: Anti-Slavery and Pro-Slavery* (Baltimore, 1863), 3, 14, 17, 23; *Speech of the Hon. A. P. Butler of South Carolina—Affairs in Kansas, March 5, 1856* (n.p., n.d.), 5.

[21] W. W. Sleigh, *Abolitionism Exposed!* (Philadelphia, 1838), 91–92; [Drayton], *South Vindicated*, 166, 276.

[22] Robert Edgar Conrad, "The Struggle for the Abolition of the Brazilian Slave Trade: 1808–1853" (Ph.D. dissertation, Columbia University, 1967), *passim;* Review of *Blackwood's* article, "Slavery and the Slave Power in the United States," *United States Review* (April, 1853), 292; Robert S. Tharin, *Arbitrary Arrests in the South; or Scenes from the Experience of an Alabama Unionist* (New York, 1863), 67, 237; Green, *Facts and Suggestions*, 86, 151.

[23] "Our Relations with England," reprinted from *Southern Literary Messenger*, VIII (June, 1842), 381, 387–88, 393–96; [Drayton], *South Vindicated*, 49, 55, 288–89; Colton, *Abolition a Sedition*, 86, 89, 90.

[24] Benton, *Thirty Years View*, 581, 586, 606. Benton refuted the charge of a British conspiracy and accused Calhoun and Green of plotting to alarm the nation in order to secure the immediate annexation of Texas.

[25] *Conspiracy Disclosed!!*, 7–9; "Periodical Press of the United States," 54–59; *United States Review* (April, 1853), 290–92; Tharin, *Arbitrary Arrests*, 237; Jacob Dewees, *To the People of Pennsylvania* (Pottsville, 1862), 8; *The Washington Despotism Dissected in Articles from "The Metropolitan Record"* (New York, 1863), pp. 75, 86. Whereas conservative Whigs perceived

abolitionism as a lethal threat to their party interests, Democrats did their best to portray the Whigs as fellow-travelers of the abolitionists.

[26] Dewees, *To the People of Pennsylvania,* 4; *Washington Despotism,* 93, 106; *Letter of Samuel Caruthers to His Constituents, Explaining His Past Action, Defining His Present Position, and the Position of Parties* (Washington, 1856), 3, 8; *Speech of the Hon. R. Hutcheson of Madison County, Delivered in the House of Representatives, March 12, 1860* (Columbus, Ohio, 1860), 3, 9–10; *Conspiracy Disclosed!!,* 6, 17; "Relative Political Status of North and South," 113, 115; Iveson L. Brooks, *A Defence of the South Against the Reproaches and Incroachments of the North* (Hamburg, S. C., 1860), 22; Sleigh, *Abolitionism Exposed,* 8.

[27] Robert Mercer Hunter, Speech of March 25, 1850, *Appendix to the Congressional Globe, for the First Session, Thirty-First Congress* (Washington, 1850), 375–76; Sydenham Moore, Speech of December 8, 1859, *The Congressional Globe . . . First Session of the Thirty-Sixth Congress* (Washington, 1860), 38–39; *Washington Despotism,* 92–94; [Drayton], *South Vindicated,* xii, 158; Brooks, *Defence of the South,* 21; Johnson, *Dual Revolutions,* 23, 33–34.

[28] *Interior Causes of the War: The Nation Demonized and Its President a Spirit-Rapper,* "By a Citizen of Ohio" (New York, 1863).

[29] "Periodical Press of the United States," 53.

[30] David Brion Davis, *The Problem of Slavery in Western Culture* (Ithaca, N.Y., 1966), especially chapters 3, 4, 10, and 13.

[31] Charles Sumner, *The Rebellion: Its Origin and Main-Spring* (Boston, 1861), 11; Sumner, *The Landmark of Freedom. Speech of Hon. Charles Sumner, Against the Repeal of the Missouri Prohibition of Slavery North of 36° 30'. In the Senate, February 21, 1854* (n.p., n.d.), 3; William Goodell (ed.), *Anti-Slavery Lecturer* (September, 1839); Theodore Parker, *A Sermon of the Dangers Which Threaten the Rights of Man in America* (Boston, 1854), 50, 53–55; Parker, *The Present Crisis in American Affairs: The Slaveholders' Attempt to Wrench the Territories from the Working People, and to Spread Bondage Over All the Land* (Boston, n.d. [1856]), 55–56.

[32] Lyman Beecher, *A Plea for the West* (2nd ed., Cincinnati, 1835), 142; Carl Schurz, "The Doom of Slavery," in *Speeches,*

Notes to Chapter 2

Correspondence and Political Papers of Carl Schurz, ed. Frederic Bancroft (New York, 1913), I, 126.

[33] Parker, *The Present Crisis*, 57; Charles Sumner, *The Slave Oligarchy and Its Usurpations, Speech of Hon. Charles Sumner, November 2, 1855, in Faneuil Hall, Boston* (n.p., n.d.), 4; [George W. Curtis], *Harper's Weekly*, V (December 7, 1861), 770; Schurz, "The Doom of Slavery," 124–31.

[34] [William Thomas] Defensor, *The Enemies of The Constitution Discovered; or, an Inquiry into the Origin and Tendency of Popular Violence* (New York, 1835), iii; George W. Curtis, *Orations and Addresses of George W. Curtis*, ed. Charles Eliot Norton (New York, 1894), I, 138; William Henry Channing, *The Civil War in America: or the Slaveholders' Conspiracy* (Liverpool, n.d. [1861]), 7, 10; John Gorham Palfrey, *Five Years' Progress of the Slave Power* (Boston, 1852), 51–52, 62.

[35] Josiah Quincy, *Address Illustrative of the Nature and Power of the Slave States* (Boston, 1856), 8; Palfrey, *Five Years' Progress*, 6–8, 32–34.

[36] Thomas, *Enemies of the Constitution, passim*; Parker, *The Present Crisis*, 61.

[37] Konrad Lorenz, *On Aggression* (New York, 1966), *passim*.

[38] Theodore Parker, *Some Thoughts on the New Assault upon Freedom in America, and the General State of the Country* (Boston, 1854), 51; Parker, *The Present Crisis*, 56.

[39] Parker, *The Dangers Which Threaten the Rights of Man*, 32; George W. Julian, *Speech of the Hon. George W. Julian, of Indiana, on the Slavery Question* (Washington, 1850), 5, 9; Henry Wilson, *The Death of Slavery Is the Life of the Nation* (Washington, 1864), 3; *Proceedings of the Rhode-Island Anti-Slavery Convention* (Providence, 1836), 30.

[40] Letter in *Proceedings of Rhode-Island Anti-Slavery Convention*, 78–79.

[41] Sumner, *The Slave Oligarchy and Its Usurpations*, 1.

Notes to Chapter 3

[1] Abraham Bishop, *Proofs of a Conspiracy Against Christianity, and the Government of the United States; Exhibited in*

Notes to Chapter 3

Several Views of the Union of Church and State in New England (Hartford, 1802).

² John C. Hamilton, *The Slave Power: Its Heresies and Injuries to the American People* (n.p., 1864), *passim*.

³ Frederick Frothingham, *Significance of the Struggle Between Liberty and Slavery in America* (New York, 1857), 6; Henry Wilson, *The Death of Slavery Is the Life of the Nation* (Washington, 1864), 5–6; Theodore Parker, *Some Thoughts on the New Assault upon Freedom in America, and the General State of the Country* (Boston, 1854), 3–7, 24, 26.

⁴ John Gorham Palfrey, *Five Years' Progress of the Slave Power* (Boston, 1852), 3–4; Joshua Leavitt, resolution reprinted in *The Friend of Man* (September 2, 1840); Augustin Cochin, *The Results of Slavery*, trans. Mary L. Booth (Boston, 1863), 9, 152.

⁵ William Goodell, *Slavery and Anti-Slavery; a History of the Great Struggle in Both Hemispheres; with a View of the Slavery Question in the United States* (New York, 1852), 320–40; William Henry Channing, *The Civil War in America: or, The Slaveholders' Conspiracy* (Liverpool, n.d. [1861]), 9; *The Slave Power: Political Tracts, No. 1* (Hartford, Conn., n.d.), 3; James C. Jackson, *The Duties and Dignities of American Freemen* (Boston, n.d.), 3; *Facts for the People. Liberty Tract No. 2* (New York, n.d.), 8–9; *Facts for the People* (Cincinnati, August, 1843), I, No. 8.

⁶ Goodell, *Slavery and Anti-Slavery*, 321–22, 327–28, 336–38; *Where Will It End? A View of Slavery in the United States in Its Aggressions and Results* (Providence, 1863), 9–10.

⁷ Charles Francis Adams, *What Makes Slavery a Question of National Concern? A Lecture, Delivered by Invitation, at New York, January 30, and at Syracuse, February 1, 1855* (n.p., n.d.), 21; Charles Sumner, *The Rebellion: Its Origin and Main-Spring* (Boston, 1861), 12.

⁸ John Elliot Cairnes, *The Slave Power: Its Character, Career and Probable Designs* (New York, 1862), 119; Wilson, *Death of Slavery*, 8; John Minor Botts, *The Great Rebellion: Its Secret History, Rise, Progress, and Disastrous Failure* (New York, 1866), 123–24; *Speech of William H. Seward, on the Kansas and Nebraska Bill, Senate of the United States, May 26, 1854* (n.p., n.d.),

5; Channing, *The Civil War in America,* 17–19, 63; Sumner, *The Rebellion,* 6.

⁹ Carl Schurz, "The Doom of Slavery," in *Speeches, Correspondence and Political Papers of Carl Schurz,* ed. Frederic Bancroft (New York, 1913), I, 130–31, 134.

¹⁰ William Seward, Address printed in *The Proceedings of the United States Anti-Masonic Convention, Held at Philadelphia, September 11, 1830* (Philadelphia, 1830), 122–23; Palfrey, *Five Years' Progress,* 11; Channing, *Civil War in America,* 30–31.

¹¹ Quoted in Alice Dana Adams, *The Neglected Period of Anti-Slavery in America, 1808–1831* (Boston, 1908), 84; Noah Porter, *Civil Liberty, A Sermon Preached in Farmington, Connecticut, July 13, 1856* (New York, 1856), 20–21; George W. Julian, "The Strength and Weakness of the Slave Power—the Duty of Anti-Slavery Men," in *Speeches on Political Questions* (New York, 1872), 73; Nathaniel P. Bailey, *Our Duty As Taught by the Agressive* [sic] *Nature of Slavery* (Akron, Ohio, 1855), 4; Charles Sumner, *The Slave Oligarchy and Its Usurpations, Speech of Hon. Charles Sumner, November 2, 1855, in Faneuil Hall, Boston* (n.p., n.d.), 8–10; Sumner, *The Rebellion,* 3–4.

¹² Charles D. Drake, *The Proclamation of Emancipation: Speech of Charles D. Drake, Delivered in Turners' Hall, St. Louis, January 28, 1863* (n.p., n.d.), 2–3; Drake, *Slavery's Destruction, the Union's Safety: Speech of Charles D. Drake, Before the Freedom Convention, in Louisville, Kentucky, February 22nd, 1864* (n.p., n.d.), 2; Frothingham, *Significance of the Struggle,* 19–20.

¹³ Theodore Parker, *The Present Crisis in American Affairs: the Slaveholders' Attempt to Wrench the Territories from the Working People, and to Spread Bondage Over All the Land* (Boston, n.d. [1856]), 57, 90–91; Julian, "Strength and Weakness of the Slave Power," 81–82; Theodore Parker, *A Sermon of the Dangers Which Threaten the Rights of Man in America* (Boston, 1854), 12, 23, 53; Drake, *Proclamation of Emancipation,* 2.

¹⁴ Parker, *Some Thoughts,* 54; *Proceedings of the Rhode-Island Anti-Slavery Convention* (Providence, 1856), 22, 62–63.

¹⁵ William Goodell (ed.), *American Jubilee,* No. 1 (March, 1854), 6–7; Parker, *Some Thoughts,* 60–61; Bailey, *Our Duty,* 18–19; Frothingham, *Significance of the Struggle,* 14–15; *Appeal of the Independent Democrats in Congress, to the People of the*

United States. Shall Slavery Be Permitted in Nebraska? (Washington, January 19, 1854), 1–2, 6.

[16] William H. Seward, *The Dangers of Extending Slavery . . . Delivered in Albany, October 12, 1855* (n.p., n.d.), 8; *Proceedings of the Rhode-Island Anti-Slavery Convention*, 67.

[17] George W. Curtis, *Orations and Addresses of George William Curtis*, ed. Charles Eliot Norton (New York, 1894), I, 128; Channing, *The Civil War*, 26; Parker, *Some Thoughts*, 29–32, 53–54.

[18] Perry Miller, *The Life of the Mind in America: From the Revolution to the Civil War* (New York, 1965), Book I; Channing, *The Civil War*, 13, 88; *Proceedings of the Rhode-Island Anti-Slavery Convention*, 54.

[19] *The Writings of Cassius Marcellus Clay*, ed. Horace Greeley (New York, 1848), 36.

[20] James G. Birney and Gamaliel Bailey (eds.), *The Philanthropist* (June 16, 1837), II; William Ellery Channing, *The Duty of the Free States, or Remarks Suggested by the Case of the Creole* (Boston, 1842), 8; Beriah Green, *The Church Carried Along, or the Opinions of a Doctor of Divinity on American Slavery* (New York), 48.

[21] Julian, "Strength and Weakness of the Slave Power," 78, 80; Enoch Hoag, *The Slave Power; or, the Spirit of Our Fathers Contrasted with the Spirit of Their Sons* (Boston, 1848), 3, 9; Palfrey, *Five Years' Progress*, 25–30, 70–74; Parker, *Dangers Which Threaten the Rights of Man*, 39–41; George Allen, *Resistance to Slavery Every Man's Duty* (Boston, 1847), 26–27.

[22] Julian, "Strength and Weakness of the Slave Power," 73, 76; Sumner, *Slave Oligarchy*, 5, 10–15; Parker, *Some Thoughts*, 35; William McMichael, *Slavery and Its Remedy* (Pittsburgh, 1856), 132.

[23] Julian, "Strength and Weakness of the Slave Power," 77.